Praise for
THE QUEEN OF CLEAN

'Linda Cobb, the self-styled Queen of Clean®, sweeps into the big time with spotless timing for a book on dirt. . . . *Talking Dirty with the Queen of Clean®* . . . has certainly cleaned up.'
– *People Magazine*

'There's no stain Linda Cobb can't tame.'
– *New York Post*

'No stain has beaten Cobb yet, and she has tried and tested almost everything. . . .'
– *The Herald* (Seattle)

'There isn't any stain or cleaning problem for which Cobb doesn't have a solution. . . .'
– *The Arizona Republic*

'Lipstick on my collar, ring around the collar? Are you kidding! Since talking with the Queen of Clean® my life has never been so clean!'
– Scott Pasmore, News Anchor,
Good Morning Arizona

'I am a huge fan of Linda Cobb, the absolutely undisputed Queen of Clean®. Our listeners love her terrific advice – and you will too! As a matter of fact, after reading this book, you may even *look forward* to doing your next load of laundry!'
– Cathy Blythe, Host, 'Problems & Solutions',
KFOR Radio, Lincoln, Nebraska

'It is comforting and refreshing to know that for once – not in our state capitals nor in Washington, DC, not in Hollywood, nor in the boardrooms of large corporations – dirt is being wiped out. Thank you, Queen of Clean®.'
– Jana Bommersbach, author, TV commentator,
and *Phoenix Magazine* columnist

Thanks for Talking Dirty Laundry with the Queen of Clean®

Talking Dirty Laundry
with the
Queen of Clean®

LINDA COBB

POCKET
BOOKS

LONDON • SYDNEY • NEW YORK • TOKYO • SINGAPORE • TORONTO

The author gratefully acknowledges and thanks the mothers and grandmothers who have passed many of these recipes down from generation to generation. These and other recipes have been collected and organized into this book. Thanks for *Talking Dirty Laundry with the Queen of Clean.*®

First published in the United States of America by Pocket Books, 2001
First published in Great Britain by Pocket Books, 2001
An imprint of Simon & Schuster UK Ltd
A Viacom Company

1 3 5 7 9 10 8 6 4 2

Simon & Schuster UK Ltd
Africa House
64–78 Kingsway
London WC2B 6AH

www.simonsays.co.uk

Simon & Schuster Australia
Sydney

A CIP catalogue record for this book is available from the British Library

ISBN 0-7434-3013-1

Printed and bound in Great Britain by
Omnia Books Ltd, Glasgow

My grateful thanks to:

My husband John, The King. Without you there would be no reason for my heart to sing, no reason to smile, no reason to laugh, and nothing to talk dirty about.

Dad, your loving smile, your gentle face, no one can fill your vacant place.

The Queen Mom. Without you there would be no Queen of Clean. Thanks for always being proud of me no matter what I did.

David and Janette; Victoria; Pat, Laura, John and Justin; Nancy and Drew; Nanette, David and Patrick, our wonderful, loving combined family. They aren't just our kids and grandchildren, they are our friends.

Betty Archambeau, who is always there with a smile and a hug.

Peggy Barker, who proves to me daily that age *is* only a state of mind.

Brenda Copeland, my editor. I think we share brain cells we are so in tune with each other. Thank you, Brenda, for your moral support, laughter, your warm heart and your dirty cleaning questions!

Beth Deveny, your moral support and hard work have been priceless.

Chuck Soderstrom, Duane Dooling and everyone at Anderson News. Thank you for your belief in the Queen and the incredible launch you gave *Talking Dirty*.

Win and Carolyn Holden. Without you I would not be 'Talking Dirty!'

Alan Centofante. You never run out of ideas or the ability to present them.

Jana Bommersbach. You are an inspiration and the yardstick I measure myself by.

Preston and Eleanor Coon. You have been the kindest, most faithful friends anyone could ever have, through the good and not so good.

All of you who continue to 'talk dirty to me!' Because of you it really *is* good to be Queen!

Contents

Contents

Foreword

Did your mum ever tell you, 'don't wash your dirty linen in public' and 'always wear clean underwear just in case you are in an accident'? The Queen Mother said it to me when I was growing up. Back then I wasn't sure what she meant. Now I think it sounds like a great lead into a laundry book!

You *can* wash your dirty linen with me – and so can your mother. In fact, I hope you will, because I'm the Queen of Clean® and I'm going to show you ways you've never thought of to keep your underwear clean . . . and everything else too!

If you are 'laundry challenged' you have come to the right place. This is where you'll find laundry basics such as how to care for your washing machine and dryer; how to choose a detergent and softener; and how to make inexpensive and effective laundry stain removers. I'm going to talk about some great laundry products, and introduce you to some of the great stain-fighting ingredients you already have in your cupboard. I'm going to give you the lowdown on ironing and dry cleaning, and I'm even going to tell you how to care for bedspreads, slipcovers and lampshades!

You're in good hands. So sit back, prop your feet up on that clothes hamper, and let's talk dirty . . . laundry, that is!

– Linda Cobb

P.S. If you have any laundry or cleaning problems you'd like me to address in my next book, just drop me a line at:

Queen of Clean® Suggestion Box
PO Box 655
Peoria, AZ 85380
USA

And don't forget to visit my website,
www.queenofclean.com

Part I
THE BASICS

Part 1

THE BASICS

1

Care and Control
of the
Washing Machine

How difficult can it be? You add water and detergent, drop in the clothes, select the cycle and walk away. When you come back the clothes are clean. Okay . . . but have you ever considered how clean your washing machine is after all that hard water and *all* those dirty clothes?

Your washer needs some TLC from time to time, especially if you have hard water in your area. So if the clothes seem dull and grey, maybe you don't need that new and improved detergent. Maybe all you need to do is clean the washing machine. Here's the easiest way I know.

Fill the washing machine with hot water. Add 1 litre

chlorine (household bleach, no detergent, please). Run the washing machine through the longest wash cycle. When the washing machine is still wet – this should be immediately after the bleach cycle – add 1 litre white vinegar and run the machine through the same cycle again. This will clean out soap scum and mineral deposits from the spin basket and also from the hoses. If you live in an area with hard water you really need to do this every three months – otherwise, every six months will do. You'll be amazed at the difference it will make.

If you start to notice little brown, rusty-looking spots on clothes when they come out of the washing machine, well, it probably *is* rust! Look your spin basket over carefully when this occurs, and check for any chips in the finish. Chipped areas rust and transfer to clothes, and the only way to remedy this problem is to replace the spin basket. Check with your appliance dealer and be sure to get the right basket for your machine. And a word of caution: take care when using detergent balls or fabric softener balls. They can chip the spin basket with their weight.

For information on removing rust stains from clothes, turn to the spotting section. It's easier than you think.

Quick Clean Method

When you don't have time to give your washing machine a really thorough clean, just fill the machine with hot water and pour in 3.8 litres white vinegar. Run through the entire wash cycle.

Cleaning the Fabric Softener Dispenser

Clean the automatic fabric softener dispenser every month to

6 weeks to keep it working well and to prevent it from leaving softener stains on clothes. (Liquid softener can leave blue spots on clothes; marks from dryer sheets can look like small grease patches.) To clean the dispenser you first must warm 250 ml white vinegar (I use the microwave), and pour it into the dispenser as you would softener. Make sure you use warm vinegar, and make sure you do this when the washing machine is empty. Large pieces of sticky fabric softener will occasionally be flushed out during cleaning, and they could adhere to clothes. Not a pretty sight. I suggest cleaning the fabric softener dispenser when you are cleaning the machine with one of the methods recommended in this chapter.

Cleaning the Bleach Dispenser

It is equally important to keep the bleach dispenser clean. Clean any removable parts by washing with hot water and washing-up liquid. When you clean the washing machine with white vinegar, be sure to add some to the bleach dispenser too.

QUICK TIP..
Use less detergent and you will have less soap buildup on clothes *and* in the washing machine. Use 115 g soda crystals and about half the amount of detergent you would usually use. Adjust this formula by increasing or decreasing detergent per your individual needs.

Tips on Buying and Placing a New Washing Machine

If you don't have space for a washing machine and dryer to sit next to each other, remember that you can buy some very efficient stackable units. Just make sure to measure the area *before* you buy.

A front-loading washing machine is definitely a space saver – the top makes a great work space for spotting clothes. You'll need to protect the top of the machine if you are going to work off it, though. A plastic breadboard is ideal.

Another good feature of front-loading machines is the way they tumble clothes. They generally tumble clothes the way a dryer does, and that's gentler on fabric than agitating. It is also less wobbly when spinning. The downside is that front-loaders generally have a smaller capacity than top-loaders, and they're usually not as good at cleaning heavy, ground-in dirt.

There are a variety of top loaders to choose from. Consider your needs carefully. You may want an extra-large capacity washer if you wash large loads of towels and sheets, but do make sure you don't overbuy. It's a waste of money to buy bells and whistles you don't need – and there's more to go wrong, too!

Give your washing machine plenty of room to vibrate. Allow a couple of centimetres of space all the way around the machine.

Important: If your washing machine's power cord does not reach the outlet, have the outlet moved or the power cord replaced with a longer one. Absolutely never use an extension cord between the power cord and the outlet. If water touches the connection between the extension cord and the power cord, you could be electrocuted.

Do not install your washing machine in an unheated garage or utility room. Water that is trapped inside can freeze and severely damage the machine.

One last installation tip: if you are installing a washing machine in a holiday home that is not heated during cold weather, have it drained completely by an appliance service technician before shutting up the home for the winter. Again, trapped water can freeze and damage the machine.

If I can leave you with a final piece of advice concerning washing machines it would be this: NEVER leave home when the washing machine is running. It only takes seconds for a hose to break or a malfunction to occur and that can cause damage and flooding in your home. I cannot tell you how many water damage cleanups we did when I owned my cleaning and disaster restoration company in Michigan. The amount of water that can pour from a small hose is unbelievable. So is the damage that can be done – not only to things that can be cleaned or replaced but also to precious treasures that can never be saved. It's heartbreaking.

2
Drying: How to Succeed Without Really Trying

Now we have the clothes washed and ready for the dryer, so let's talk dirty dryers!

Keeping the dryer clean is important: a clean dryer will work more efficiently, saving you time and money. A clean dryer will also help to prevent dryer fires. Dryer fires are much more common than you might think, so avoid them at all costs.

First the basics:

If you have a lint-clogged dryer venting system, your clothes will not dry properly and you will waste time and money running longer cycles to get the clothes completely dry. Turn the dryer on, and go outside and hold your hand under the dryer vent hood – you know, that metal thing on the outside of the house. If you don't feel a strong flow of air it's time to clean.

Clean the dryer vent pipe or flex exhaust hose once a year to prevent lint buildup. Try to lock a date in your mind and do it every year. I like Halloween 'cause you can extract the lint and create a dust bunny costume at the same time! Remove the duct or hose from the dryer back and the exhaust mounting, and shake it out. It may be necessary to run an old cloth through the hose to dislodge any lint that is unwilling or unable to leave the vent. Be sure to reseal the joints, using a fresh piece of duct tape if necessary.

While you have the dryer out, vacuum and wash the floor area underneath the unit. If you see any grease or oil leaks on the floor, it's time to call the appliance repairman.

On the outside of the vent, clean the hood and vent by using a straightened wire coat hanger or bottle-type brush. Push it back and forth in the vent to remove accumulated lint.

Always make sure that your vent is straight. Kinks will block the airflow.

The lint filter in the dryer is no less important than the vent. Keeping it clean is vital. A clogged lint filter allows lint to accumulate and can eventually start a fire. A dirty lint filter also blocks airflow, so your clothes will take longer to dry. And that means extra money on your gas or electric bill.

To clean the filter, remove it, wipe off the lint and replace. You can do this easily by wiping the filter with a used dryer fabric softener sheet, which will collect the accumulated lint so that you can dispose of it without additional mess.

It's important to vacuum the filter periodically, and to clean the area where the lint filter is installed with vacuum attachments. (This is the opening on the dryer that the filter slides into.)

Important: If you have a gas dryer, always use caution not to kink or damage the gas line when shifting.

Dryer Dilemmas

Now that you know how to clean the dryer, it's time to talk about some quick, easy tips to make your job a lot easier. Anyone who does laundry knows how those little OOPS! can happen and how frustrating they can be. So let's de-oops the clothes dryer!

Lint-Free Drying

If you're drying clothes that have lint – or a big oops, a tissue has gone through the washing machine – put a piece of nylon net in the dryer along with the clothes. The net will catch the lint effectively so you won't have to drag out the lint roller, or worse still, pick off all of the fuzz. I buy cheap nylon net from a fabric store and throw it out when it's full of lint.

Oops! I Forgot to Take the Clothes Out of the Dryer

We all know that if you take items out of the dryer as soon as it shuts off, you can fold or hang your clothes with little or no ironing. But you can't always get to the dryer immediately.

Let's be honest. How many times have you gone to the dryer and found a load of clothes that were forgotten? Oops! The clothes are a mass of wrinkles! Don't go to the trouble of rewashing the clothes, and don't iron them, either. Just toss a damp towel in the dryer and rerun the load for a few minutes. The wrinkles will release and you can hang up the clothes. Remember, though, never use a white towel with dark clothes or you will give yourself another problem . . . lint!

Yikes! How Did That Get in the Dryer?

To remove crayon, lipstick or lip salve from the dryer, turn it off and spray a paper towel with WD-40 Lubricant®. Wipe out the dryer until all of the mess is removed. Wash out with warm water and washing-up liquid, then dry a load of old wet rags.

Try Stain Devil to remove chewing gum and glue. For ink, use surgical spirit or Stain Devil 4.

Don't Even Think of Putting That in the Dryer!

Don't put stained or spotted clothes in the dryer. The heat will set the stain, making it next to impossible to remove. Re-treat the stain with one of the appropriate methods mentioned in this book, and launder again.

Important: Do not put anything in the dryer that has come in contact with paint, petrol, oil used on machinery, etc., or any flammable fluids. These things are fire hazards and the fumes they give off can ignite. If they come in contact with a hot dryer you could have a serious problem. Line dry these items.

DRYER QUICK TIPS ....

- Clean the dryer lint filter after each use.
- Always check to see that the dryer is empty before using.
- Avoid drying extremely small loads or crowding the dryer with extra large loads. Very small loads can clump, and very large loads don't tumble well. Both waste time and energy.
- Dry lightweight fabrics together and heavy fabrics together for more efficient drying.
- Dry loads one after another. That way you can utilize the heat already in the dryer.
- Don't add wet clothes to clothes that are almost dry. This wastes energy — and money!

3

Getting the Hang of Line Drying

We have come full circle. For years it seemed like the dryer had taken over and that clotheslines were obsolete. Now, we are returning to the days of natural fabrics, with drip-dry clothes, clothes that need to be laid flat to dry, and clothes that cannot be put in the dryer for any reason. Don't worry. You don't need a clothesline in the garden to care for some of these hang-to-dry clothes.

The Basics

As your grandma will tell you, don't spin out too much water from clothes that you are going to hang to dry: that sets in the wrinkles. Instead, shut off the washing machine halfway through the spin cycle and hang the clothes on a clothesline, allowing for plenty of air circulation between clothes. Dry coloured clothes out of direct sunlight (the sun fades them), but hang white clothes in the sun – this will bleach them to an incredible, eye-popping white. They'll smell great too.

Hanging clothes on plastic hangers with sloped ends will allow them to dry without those awful 'shoulder dimples'. You'll avoid rust that way too!

Specific Drying Tips

Trousers: Hang these by the cuffs. The weight of the trousers will usually keep the legs wrinkle-free, which means less or no pressing. We like that!

Sweaters: To prevent sweaters from having 'shoulder dimples' or 'clothespin points', thread the legs of an old pair of panty hose through the arms of the sweater, and pull the waist out through the neck. Attach pegs to the feet and waist of the panty hose instead of the sweater. Just make sure to remove the panty hose before you put on the sweater. Unless you plan to rob a bank . . .

Dresses and coats: When hanging heavy dresses and coats to dry, use two hangers to absorb the weight. If hanging them outside to dry, hook the two hangers in the opposite direction to keep the breeze from blowing the garment off the line.

Lingerie and panty hose: These are better dried in the house over the shower bar, on a small bathroom clothesline, or from plastic hangers with clips.

Handy Hints

- If you do use a clothesline outside, remember to keep it clean by washing it periodically.

- Strong sun will eventually weaken fibres, so keep an eye on the clothes and bring them in as soon as they are dry.

- Bedding washed and hung out to dry occasionally will be crisp and fresh-smelling. White linens will be brighter!

- Do not air-dry down duvets. They dry too slowly and mould or mildew may form in the process.

- A tension curtain rod hung in a laundry room makes a great place to hang clothes to dry. A piece of chain also works well, and you can hook hangers through the links.

- If a garment label says 'hang to dry', don't put it in the dryer. It may shrink or the fibres may distort.

- If clothes are wrinkled after line drying, putting them in the dryer on the 'no heat' or 'air fluff' setting may save you from ironing them. (Do not use a fabric softener sheet, though. Without heat, fabric softener sheets can stain clothes.)

4

Laundry Detergents and Great Alternatives

I don't think there is a greater laundry challenge than walking down the soap and detergent aisle and deciding what products to buy. We are constantly bombarded with ads about how well this one cleans, how well that one smells . . . this one contains bleach, that one contains optic brighteners, and that one over there . . . well, it contains every cleaning agent known to man – and woman. Argh! But what really matters in a laundry detergent? When is more just too much?

I have a rule that I follow with laundry detergent, and it's this: less is more. When I want a laundry detergent or soap I want that and only that. Period. I want to be the one who determines when I need bleach, softener or other additives, so I opt for the simplest product that basically does one thing: removes and suspends soil from my clothes and leaves them clean and fresh. Now by *fresh,* I don't mean have a smelly odour after the wash. I like to leave the house without advertising what detergent I use by the way I smell. I like the labels that read 'FREE'. I don't want odour or artificial colour, just the cleaning product. It is healthier for the body and the clothes. If I want to have a fragrance, I will choose the perfume. I don't want to smell like combinations of soap and softener and other laundry products all mixed together.

Basic laundry detergent: This is where it all starts. Choose your laundry product (bear in mind my lecture above), and measure it into the machine. Remember to adjust the amount of detergent used to the size of your load. (You may need to adjust the amount if you have hard water.) More is not better where laundry soap is concerned. It's just harder to rinse out. Detergent residue makes fabric sticky, and that makes it attract soil faster.

I've tested all laundry detergents, and believe me, that was a challenge. Sometimes the detergent that gets out the most spills and spots is not the one that is best for your clothes, or your family. Some laundry detergents are particularly hard on coloured fabrics, fading them and giving dark colours a whitish cast.

I think it is worth doing your own testing to find the best detergent for your needs.

I am a liquid soap kind of Queen, because I like to measure out my detergent in the cap, and then do a little prespotting with it before I toss the clothes and the balance of the detergent in the machine.

Laundry additives: If you have a particularly soiled load of clothes and feel that your detergent needs a kick, try a safe additive like Ace 'wash booster'. It removes soils and stains, brightens clothes and freshens laundry without an artificial smell. It is also suitable on delicate fabrics such as wool and silk.

Laundry borax is great for nappies. It's completely safe for baby clothes and hand washables. It's also a great deodorizer and has more uses in cleaning than I can name.

Allergy-free products: Many people, particularly children, have allergies and asthma problems which seem to be directly related to the cleaning and laundry products we use in our homes. If your family appears to be allergic to its underwear (no, I'm not kidding), it may be your detergent. I've been researching allergy-free, nontoxic cleaning products for a long time, and I'm happy to tell you that I have found environmentally friendly products that work to avoid these reactions. I've tested these products. They work safely on laundry for the whole family, babies to adults.

The following products are made by a company called Soapworks (see their website: www.soapworks.com). They were created by a woman in direct response to her son's severe, life-threatening asthma.

Try the Fresh Breeze Laundry Powder™ or the Fresh Breeze Liquid™. It is made from natural ingredients such as coconut and palm kernel soap. This can be used to safely spot clothes and presoak too, and has a light, fresh scent of natural ginger.

They also make Sun Shine Liquid Soap™ for dishes and washing delicates, and again, it is all natural.

In Chapter 8, I'll tell you about Soapworks Brilliant Bleach™, which is a hydrogen peroxide-based bleach.

There is something for everyone in the laundry aisle, but a word of caution: not all clothes require those heavy-duty products. They can be hard on fabrics and on the environment. Grandma didn't need those additives, and her clothes lasted a long time.

5

Be a Spot Hot Shot!

I love natural products, and I love things that I can make for pennies and still have them work better than the products I could buy at the store. Here are some of my favourite laundry spot removers. Use them just as you would over-the-counter products, but take note: many of them are designed to take care of specific spots and stains.

Start with a clean spray and/or squeeze bottle, and always be sure to label any product you make. It's important to know what the bottle contains and what it was intended for. I like to include the recipe on the label too – that way I can mix up additional product with ease. Cover the label with clear packaging tape or a piece of clear adhesive sheet to protect the label from moisture.

These spotters are all intended for washable fabrics. If in doubt, test in an inconspicuous spot, such as a seam.

General All-Purpose Laundry Spotter

Combine the following to make a generic spotter that works on a wide variety of stains:

    1 part surgical spirit

    2 parts water

If you use a large spray bottle you can add 1 bottle of surgical spirit and 2 of the spirit bottles filled with water. Spray this on spots and spills, wait a few minutes, and then launder as usual.

Beverage, Fruit and Grass Remover

Combine equal portions of:

    white vinegar

    washing-up liquid

    water

Shake well and work the solution into the spot. Let stand a few minutes and then launder as usual.

Non-oily Stain Remover

Combine equal portions of the following ingredients:

    ammonia

    washing-up liquid

    water

Shake well, and work the solution into the spot. Let stand a few minutes and flush with water. This solution works well on stains such as milk, blood, perspiration and urine. *Do not use on washable wool, silk, spandex, acrylic and acetate.*

Oily Stain Remover

Combine the following:

1 tablespoon glycerin

1 tablespoon washing-up liquid

8 tablespoons of water

Work the solution into grease and oil stains. Let sit a few minutes, flush with water and launder as usual.

Again, remember all of these spotters are for washable fabrics only and none of them are for silk, wool, spandex, acrylic and acetate. When in doubt, test first!

6
Bringing Out the Big Guns

It's time to talk about the big guns of laundry spotters. We all need them from time to time. But what's best? What really works? Read on. I've tried them all, so you won't have to!

A quick disclaimer: remember, I am counting on you to test a small, inconspicuous area on the fabric for colourfastness *before* you use any of these spotters. Don't let laundry spotters dry. Launder soon after spotting to prevent the spot from becoming a stain. Don't let me down!

Dylon Stain Remover 3: This is a terrific 'can't be without' spotter for dry-clean-only clothes. Blot it on until the stain is gone and then blow-dry to avoid a ring.

Fairy Mild Green Household Soap: This is that old-fashioned green bar soap that your grandmother used and it's a great spotter for numerous spots and stains. Wet the bar and simply rub the stain, working it in well. Let it sit a few minutes. This spotter still works even if allowed to dry on the fabric. Great for ring-around-the-collar and perspiration stains.

Stain Devil: Ink and marker can be a challenge to remove, but this product really proves its worth. Follow package directions carefully and be sure to read the list of things *not* to use it on *before* you start. Also available for more specific stains. You squeeze the solution on to the stain, work it in with your fingertips, leave for five to ten minutes (do not allow to dry out), then rinse under warm running water rubbing the fabric to remove the stain.

Spot Shot Instant Carpet Stain Remover®: This one wins the prize for the most unusual laundry spotter, but it's *still* one of the Queen's favourite products. Yes, that's right, it's not just for carpet. It's also a great laundry prewash spotter – and boy does it work. It is safe for all colourfast washables and works in all wash temperatures. Spray the stained area thoroughly, saturating the stain. If the stain is difficult or stubborn, work it between your thumbs. Allow Spot Shot® to sit at least 60 seconds, then launder as usual. *Do not* allow it to dry on the fabric and do not use it on silks, fabrics labeled 'dry clean only' or noncolourfast fabrics. This product works on oily stains, ink, pet stains, cola, shoe polish, lipstick, blood and others. A must-have in the laundry room.

7

Stain Removers That Are Hiding in Your Cupboard

You may not know this, but some of the very best spot and stain removers are things you use every single day! Not only do these stain removers work great – they're right at your fingertips!

Ammonia: The perspiration stain fighter.

Bicarbonate of soda: Removes odours.

Cream of tartar: I bet you have some of this in the kitchen cupboard, but how often do you use it? Well, here's your chance. Mix cream of tartar with lemon juice and you have a wonderful bleach for white clothes spotted with food or other stains. It's even effective on many rust stains.

Denture-cleaning tablets: The cure-all for white table linens with food stains and white cotton with stains. Dissolve one tablet per 125 ml water. Pour directly on stain or spot.

Dishwasher detergent: Keep this on hand as a bleach substitute and whitener/brightener even if you *don't* have a dishwasher. Liquid, powder and tablet form all work well. If you choose the tablet, make sure it has dissolved before you add clothes. Pour directly on stain, or soak.

Glycerin: You can remove tar, tree sap (think Christmas tree), juice stains, mustard, ketchup and barbecue sauce.

Hydrogen peroxide: 3 per cent hydrogen peroxide is super for removing blood stains, especially if they are fairly fresh. It also is a wonderful bleaching agent for stubborn stains on white clothes. Combine 100 ml hydrogen peroxide and 1 teaspoon of ammonia for an unbeatable stain removal combination. Make sure to use 3 per cent and *not* the kind you use to bleach your hair!

Lemon Juice: This is nature's bleach and disinfectant. I don't know where we'd be without it. If you have spots on white clothes, apply some lemon juice and lay them in the sun. Apply a little more lemon juice prior to laundering, or prespray and launder as usual. This is really effective on baby formula stains.

Meat tenderizer: A combo of meat tenderizer (unseasoned, please, or you'll have a whole new stain!) and cold water is just the answer to protein-based stains such as blood, milk, etc.

Salt: Sprinkling salt on spilled red wine will keep the wine from staining until you can launder it. Mixed with lemon juice, salt will remove mildew stains.

Shampoo: Any brand will do. Cheap is fine. I save the small bottles from hotel/motel stays and keep them in the laundry room. Great for treating ring-around-the-collar, mud and cosmetic stains.

Shaving cream: That innocent-looking can of shaving cream in your bathroom is one of the best spot and stain removers available. That's because it's really whipped soap! If you have a spill on your clothes (or even your carpet), moisten the spot, work in some shaving cream, and then flush it with cool water. If the offending spot is on something you're wearing, work the shaving cream in and then use a clean cloth (a flannel works fine) to blot the shaving cream and the spot away. A quick touch of the hair-dryer to prevent a ring and you're on your way. The best thing about shaving cream is that even if it doesn't work it won't set the stain, so the spot can still be removed later. Keep a small sample can in your suitcase when you travel. It's saved me more than once!

Soda water: My favourite *Oh my gosh, how did I do that?* spotter. Use it on any fabric or surface that can be treated with water. A slight dabbing on dry-clean-only fabrics is also permissible, just be sure to test first! Use soda water on any spill – ask the waiter for some if you're dining out – dab it on and blot it off. Soda water keeps spills from becoming stains and brings the offending spill to the surface so it can be easily removed. It's totally safe. I always make sure to have a bottle on hand.

Surgical spirit: Great for grass stains and so much more.

Washing-up liquid: A wonderful spotter, used undiluted on tough stains.

WD-40 Lubricant®: Check out your garage or the 'fix-it' cupboard. If you don't have any, pick up a can the next time you're at the hardware store. Why? Because we've all had those nasty grease stains and oil stains on clothes: salad dressing misses the salad and gets the blouse, or grease splatters when you are cooking – or crayon/lipstick/lip salve gets on your clothes! WD-40 is your answer. Spray some on, wait 10 minutes, then work in undiluted washing-up liquid and launder as usual. Works well on everything *except* silk!

White vinegar: A great spotter for suede – used undiluted. It's also a wonderful fabric softener. Just put 50 ml white vinegar in the final rinse. (And no, you won't smell like a salad!)

It's worthwhile to keep these things on hand. As you can see, most are inexpensive *and* have other uses. They'll make you the laundry Queen – or King! – in your home.

8

Bleach 101:
Whiter Whites,
Brighter Brights

Are you one of those people who thinks that directions are what you read to find out what you did wrong? Then pay attention. I'm going to give you my dos and don'ts of bleach basics.

DO ....

- Read the directions on the container of bleach.

- Check the labels on the fabric you wish to bleach.

- Test the bleach if you are unsure. To do this with chlorine (household) bleach, mix 1 tablespoon of chlorine bleach with 50 ml cold water. Find a hidden area on the piece of clothing and place a drop of the solution on it. Leave this for a minute or two and then blot to determine if there is any colour change.

- To test all-fabric bleaches, mix 1 teaspoon of the bleach with 250 ml hot water. Again, place a drop on an inconspicuous area. Wait at least 15 minutes, blot, and check for any change in the colour.

- Of course if any colour change takes place you won't want to use that type of bleach on that type of fabric.

- Always be sure to rinse bleach out of fabric thoroughly.

DON'TS ....

- Absolutely never allow undiluted chlorine (household) bleach to come in contact with fabrics.

- Never use any kind of bleach directly on fabric without testing it first.

- Never use more bleach than called for. It can damage fabrics and is wasteful too.

- *NEVER* use chlorine (household) bleach and ammonia in the same wash! It can generate deadly fumes.

Now let's talk about the bleaches one by one.

Chlorine Bleach

The strongest, fastest-acting bleach available, chlorine (household) bleach is very effective on cottons, linens and some synthetics when used properly. Used improperly it can weaken cloth fibres, causing them to disintegrate. It can even cause holes. Always follow container directions with care, and never use chlorine bleach on silk, wool, spandex, acetate, fibres treated to be flame-resistant or dry-clean-only fabrics.

Most of us have had a bad experience with chlorine bleach, so use care. Never pour it on hand washables, and never pour it on to clothes that are in the washing machine. Pour it in the bleach dispenser, if your washing machine is so equipped, or into the washer while it is filling with water *before* adding the clothes. For hand washables, dilute it prior to adding the clothes and be sure to adjust the amount accordingly for the amount of water being used.

Name brands and store brands work the same, so purchase the product of your choice, or the one with the best price.

All-Fabric Bleach or Oxygen Bleach

This is a much milder form of bleach that works well on delicate fabrics or those requiring gentle care. It is slower-acting than chlorine bleach and is less effective in restoring whiteness to fabrics. It may be effective, though, through regular use. This bleach can be used on all fabrics, even silks, as long as the manufacturer's care tag does not say 'no bleach'. Add this bleach at the same time you add your detergent and do not pour directly on the clothes. More is not better, so measure, don't just pour.

A New Generation of Bleach

Soapworks (see their website: www.soapworks.com) has come up with a new generation of bleach that is effective, user friendly, and safe for use by people with allergies and asthma. It is hypoallergenic, nontoxic, biodegradable, 100 per cent natural, safe for septic tanks, contains no chemicals, no dyes and no fragrances.

This product is called Brilliant™, and it is just that! Created with hydrogen peroxide – which is the safest, natural whitener and brightener for fabrics – this bleach can be used effectively on whites and coloured fabrics both. Clothes can be soaked safely for 24 hours or more without harm to either fabric or colour.

Brilliant™ is also a softener, so no additional softening agent is required. Add 50 ml to the washing machine as it fills with water. As with any bleach product, test in an inconspicuous area when in doubt.

Making Your Own Bleaching Agents

Yes, you *can* create your own forms of bleach with things you already have at home.

Lemon juice: Nature's bleach and disinfectant, lemon juice can be used to whiten clothes.

Take 3.8 litres of the hottest water possible for the fabric you're bleaching and add 100 ml bottled lemon juice or the slices of one or two lemons. Soak the clothes for 30 minutes or even overnight. This works especially well on white socks and underwear, and is safe for polyester fabrics. Don't use on silks, though.

Dishwasher detergent: This is another wonderful bleaching agent for white clothes. Fill a bucket with the hottest possible water for the fabric you are working with, and add 2 tablespoons of any brand of dishwasher detergent. Soak white clothes for 30 minutes or even overnight. Dump into the washing machine and launder with your detergent as usual.

To use this bleaching technique in the washing machine, fill the machine with water and add 55–115 g dishwasher detergent. Agitate for several minutes and then add clothes. Soak as directed above and then add detergent and launder as usual.

Hydrogen peroxide: This can be used to bleach delicate items such as wool or wool blends. Soak them overnight in a solution of one part 3 per cent hydrogen peroxide to eight parts cold water. Launder according to care directions.

9
Fabric Softeners – The Soft Sell

abric softeners are used to make fabrics soft and fluffy, and to minimize static cling. They can also reduce wrinkling and make ironing easier.

Liquid softeners: These should be added to the final rinse cycle by the automatic dispenser (if your washing machine has one), or by hand if not. Carefully follow the directions on the label, and make sure to measure: too much is not better, nor is too little.

If using an automatic dispenser, add the softener then follow with an equal amount of water to help disperse the liquid softener. This will also help to eliminate softener spots on clothes.

Dryer-added softeners: These paper-thin sheets soften clothes, and they also work with the heat of the dryer to reduce static electricity in the load – which means that your dress won't cling to your panty hose and your trousers won't cling to your socks! I find store brands work just as well as higher-priced varieties, so go ahead and make your choice by fragrance or price. Whatever suits you.

By the way, if static cling is a problem (and it happens to the best of us), try smoothing your skirt with a damp pair of hands. A little bit of hand cream on top of your panty hose works well, too.

A word of advice. Dryer softener sheets can cause buildup on towels, and that can make them feel slippery and reduce their absorbency. Use the softener only once every two to three washings to avoid this.

Retired Softener Sheets

Once you have used the pesky little sheet, remember my earlier advice: use it to clean off the lint filter in the dryer before you toss it. Here are some other uses for those retired sheets.

• If you have a casserole or pan with burned-on food, fill with hot water, toss in a softener sheet for several hours (overnight is fine), and the burned-on food will slide right out.

• Run a needle and thread through the sheet to prevent static from tangling the thread.

• Wipe the television screen, venetian blinds or any other surface that attracts dust with a used sheet to reduce the static electricity that attracts dust.

• Place a used sheet in luggage, drawers, cupboards, dustbins, under car seats and in your laundry bag or hamper to provide a fresh scent.

• Tuck a used sheet into shoes before placing them in your luggage. Shoes will smell fresh and you can use the dryer softener sheet to buff shoes and remove dust after wearing.

• Polish chrome to a brilliant shine after cleaning.

• Use it to wrap Christmas ornaments or other fragile things before boxing for storage. The dryer sheet will protect them and you can wipe Christmas ornaments prior to hanging on the tree to reduce static electricity and repel dust.

• Wipe car dashboards with a used sheet to shine and repel dust.

Retired dryer fabric softener sheets have plenty of uses left, so don't waste them. And don't use new softener sheets for any of these purposes. Pick up a *used* or, as I like to call them, *retired,* sheet instead! I put my used dryer sheets in an empty tissue box I keep in the laundry room. This way they are always handy.

Making Your Own Dryer Fabric Softener Sheets

Believe it or not, you can make your own dryer fabric softener sheets. Simply take an old flannel, mist it with 1 part of your favourite liquid fabric softener and 2 parts water, then toss it in the dryer with the clothes. Re-mist for each new load of clothes and occasionally launder it when doing towels to remove any softener buildup and soften the towels at the same time.

I keep a mixture in a small spray bottle on the shelf in the laundry room along with a few old flannels. I find that 75 ml liquid fabric softener and 150 ml warm water makes a good quantity. Shake prior to spraying on the flannel, and *always* label the bottle of any mixture you make yourself to keep it from accidentally being misused.

If your detergent already contains softener (read the label) you may not need additional softener unless you are getting a lot of static cling in your clothes.

Fabric Softener Spots on Clothes

No matter how hard you try, at some point you will probably pull out a load of clothes and find either blue spots from liquid fabric softener or 'grease'-type spots from dryer softener sheets on your clothes. Here's what to do:

Liquid softener spots: If spotting occurs, wet the item and rub with undiluted washing-up liquid, then rewash. Wetting and rubbing with shampoo seems to work too. Do *not* rub with laundry detergent. It won't remove the spot – in fact, it may set it in.

If liquid softener has been allowed to freeze, dissolve the required amount of softener with warm water before adding to the wash.

Dryer fabric softener sheet spots: If spotting occurs, rub the area with a wet bar of soap, such as Dove®, and then relaunder.

To avoid spots, place the sheet on top of the clothes in the dryer rather than mixing it in, and start the dryer immediately. Do not use the sheet when you are using the air fluff cycle without heat.

Important: Do *not* use dryer sheets on children's sleepwear or other garments labelled as flame-resistant as they may reduce flame resistance. These sheets are *not* nontoxic, so keep out of reach of children and pets to avoid accidental ingestion.

10

The Hard Truth About Water Softeners

If you live in an area that has hard water you will be well acquainted with the greying or yellowing effect that hard water minerals can have on your clothes. You may also have noticed that, rather than suds in your washing machine, you have grey-looking water and, sometimes, scum on the water surface.

Not sure if you have hard water? You can check your local water supply office – they will tell you the degree of hardness in your water. If you have well water you might want to call a water treatment company. They'll be able to test your supply. Of course, you can also look out for these telltale signs:

- Fabrics look dull and grey.

- Fabrics feel stiff instead of soft.

- Soaps and detergents don't lather well.

- White residue appears around drains, taps and on glassware.

If your water is not too hard (less than 10.6 grains of hardness per 3.8 litres), you can help alleviate the problems associated with hard water by adjusting the amount of detergent you use. Again, start by using half the amount of detergent called for. You can also give your detergent a 'kick' by using soda crystals or laundry borax along with your detergent, following package directions. These products are found in the laundry additive aisle at the grocery store or at discount stores. If you find that your clothes still do not have the degree of cleanness and softness that you desire, you may need to try a liquid softener that you can add to your laundry along with your detergent, or go to a mechanical means of softening.

MakingYour Own Water Softener

Combine the following in a labelled container. Plastic milk bottles, washed well, work great.

     225 g soda crystals
     115 g laundry borax
     3.8 litres warm water

To use: Add 250 ml of the solution to each load of wash water along with your normal laundry detergent.

If you still find that your wash is dingy and you are not

getting any lather from your bar soap in the shower, then you may need to turn to a mechanical softener which is attached to the house water system.

11

Starch and Sizing

Starches and speedy or easy iron restore body to fabrics that have become limp through washing or dry cleaning. They also form a protective barrier to repel dirt. Fabrics such as cotton or linen respond particularly well to these products.

Starch: Comes in spray, liquid and powder form. Liquid and powder starch should be combined with water – the directions on the package will tell you what proportions to use. Mix to a thick paste if you want your clothes to have a crisp starched appearance. A thinner consistency will give you a lighter look. You can also add starch to the final machine rinse if you like. Just be sure to follow the directions carefully.

The easiest form of starch is spray starch, which you apply while ironing. Just spritz it on the clothes and iron. It's that easy! Spray starches provide a light effect. Use powder or liquid if you prefer a heavier starch.

Speedy or easy iron: A lighter cousin to starch, this helps to combat the effect on clothes from general wear, moisture, perspiration, and washing or dry cleaning. Buy it in a spray can and spritz it on garments as you iron.

Do not use too much of these spray products. And don't use your iron on a high heat – it will flake off if you do.

⑫

Cry Me a River — The Colour Ran!

Ever turned your underwear pink? Then you know what I'm talking about when I say that some dark colours bleed during initial washing. Not all colours are what we call 'colourfast', so you must be careful to prevent the dye of one garment from running on to another.

Is It Colourfast?

How do you know if an item is colourfast? Test it! Try this simple colourfast test before you launder new fabrics. You'll save yourself a lot of time and heartache if you do.

• Place a drop of water on an inside seam or another inconspicuous spot. Blot with a white cotton wool ball or towel.

• If the cotton wool ball remains clean, it is safe to wash with other clothes. If it picks up some colour from the fabric then you must wash the garment separately.

Be careful not to drip-dry fabrics that are not colourfast. The colour can streak. Instead, roll these clothes in a towel to absorb excess moisture, then hang to dry, away from other fabrics.

Uh-Oh . . .

What happens if a pair of new black socks were somehow washed with your favourite white blouse? Fugitive colour happens, that's what! Don't despair. Some products can help you do away with colour runs.

Colour Run Removers: Three useful products are Dylon Colour Run for handwashing whites and some coloureds, Dylon Colour Safe Colour Run Remover for machine washing whites and coloureds and Rescue Colour Run Remover for washable colourfast and dry clean fabrics. All are available at supermarkets. You *must* test the fabric to be sure that it's colourfast, otherwise the garment's original colour will be removed along with the fugitive colour. Follow the directions carefully and use great care.

Dylon Colour Seal This unique treatment permanently seals in colour on most washable fabrics and will keep colours looking new. You should use *before* washing a garment that is likely to bleed. Just think of this as an ounce of prevention. Again, as with everything, try in an inconspicuous area first and read the directions carefully.

Important: These products contain chemicals that can be harmful to children and pets, so please make sure to take adequate storage precautions.

⓭
You Can Be a Rescuer of Things That Reek!

Odour can be a big laundry problem. There are a number of perfumed products that claim to remove odour and leave fabric fresh-smelling. It's been my experience, however, that most of these products just mask smells. I don't know about you, but I'd rather not have lilac-scented perspiration.

Putting white vinegar in the final rinse will remove some odours. But for difficult odours, such as smoke, urine, pet, garlic, petrol, etc., you need a much stronger product. I highly recommend ODORZOUT™, a 100 per cent natural product with no odour of its own (see their website:

www.88stink.com). Use it dry or wet. It doesn't cover-up odours – it actually absorbs them! And it's safe for people with asthma or allergies too!

To use dry, sprinkle directly on clothes that have an offensive odour, and allow them to sit for several hours. Intense odours, such as petrol, can be treated for several days with no harm to the fabric. Just make sure you allow air to circulate – the product won't work in an enclosed space.

To use wet, simply fill the washing machine and add 1 to 2 teaspoons of ODORZOUT™. Agitate for a minute and then add the clothes and your detergent. Launder as usual.

ODORZOUT™ is great when sprinkled on pet bedding several hours before laundering. You can also use it to control odour in linen baskets and nappy buckets. It is safe and nontoxic for use around kids and pets, which is a big plus.

Try the ODORZOUT™ Pouch as well. You can put them in empty shoes to eliminate smells, and in cupboards and drawers to keep odours at bay. I love the convenience.

Remember, if it stinks, it's best to treat it immediately, before the odour can be passed on to other items.

14

Care Labels: What Are They Good For?

When you examine a label, do you look at the size and nothing else? Well, you're missing out on a lot of valuable information. Care labels are very important. You should read each and every one of them before you purchase a garment, and each time you have it cleaned.

The EU requires manufacturers to attach a permanent label to textile garments indicating directions for care. This label must be easily located. It should not separate from the garment, and it should remain legible during the lifespan of the garment. The label must warn about any part of the recommended care method that would harm the garment or other garments being laundered or dry cleaned with it. It must also specify if a garment cannot be cleaned without damage.

Symbols may also appear on a care label to supplement written instructions. When a garment carries an international symbol tag, all care methods will usually be listed.

May I Remove the Care Label? Garments are required by law to have a care label attached at the time of sale. Of course, no law can take into account a woman wearing a little black dress with a big white care label hanging out the back. Removing the care tag does entail some risk, though; you may forget the proper cleaning instructions and your dry cleaner will not have access to some valuable information.

If you do remove care labels, mark them with a description of the item and put them in a safe place where they can be easily located. You might remember today that your favourite summer dress should be washed in cold water and laid flat to dry, but by next summer you may have forgotten this entirely. A corkboard in the laundry room is wonderful. Care directions will be at your fingertips and at those of other family members who may surprise you by doing the laundry sometime. Remove labels from the board when you no longer have the item.

Cleaning Instructions

Dry clean: A garment marked 'dry clean only' can be cleaned using normal dry-cleaning fluid found in any commercial or coin-operated dry-cleaning establishment. Be aware that dry cleaning, despite its name, is not necessarily dry. Water may be involved in the process, whether by moisture added to the fluid, or by steam press or steam air-form finishing.

Professionally dry clean: If your garment is marked 'professionally dry clean', then it is restricted to the dry-cleaning methods possible only in commercial dry-cleaning plants. A label marked 'professionally dry clean' may be accompanied by further information, such as symbols that specify use of a particular solvent. Garments marked with F, for example, should be cleaned in perchlorethylene – good dry cleaners will know how to moderate the solution for the correct result on a particular fabric.

Machine wash: Indicates use of either a commercial or home washing machine. Other information may be included, such as specific washing temperatures, size of load or drying instructions.

Does 'washable' mean it can also be dry-cleaned? If a garment care label says 'washable' it may be safely dry-cleaned – and it may not! Unfortunately, there is no way of telling from the label. A manufacturer is required to list only one safe method of cleaning, no matter how many other methods can be safely employed. And be warned: manufacturers are not required to alert you to care procedures that *may not* be safe.

15

Doing the Laundry Sorting Boogie

Now that we have our products ready to spot, bleach, launder and soften, it's time to actually do the laundry! Make it easy on yourself. Sort *before* you start to wash.

Some people like the 'grab and stuff' laundry method: grab the clothes – no matter what fabric or colour – and stuff them into the machine, as many as you can at one time. These people are easy to recognize. They're the ones with pink underwear, colour-streaked clothes, shrunken sweaters, short trousers, and clothes that are otherwise 'challenged'.

Sort your laundry for best results. You'll thank me for this advice, I assure you.

Separate

- Dark fabrics from white and light-coloured fabrics.
- Lightly soiled clothes from heavily soiled garments such as work clothes.
- Fabrics by water temperature (hot – warm – cold).
- Fabrics that will shed lint on other fabrics (terrycloth, corduroy, etc.).
- Lingerie, hose and delicate fabrics that should be washed in a mesh bag.
- Clothes that may have fugitive colour and bleed on to others.

Do This *Before* You Wash

- Button buttons.
- Hook bras.
- Zip zips.
- Tie sashes, cords, straps etc., to prevent tangling.
- Check pockets for coins, tissues, pens, etc.
- Remove anything on the garment that cannot be washed.
- Repair tears so they don't become larger while agitating.

Now It's Time to Pretreat

- Check for spots, spills, stains, etc., before putting a load of clothes into the washing machine.
- Pretreat these with one of the spotters you'll find in Chapters 5 and 6, or go to the stain removal guide for help.

• Soak heavily soiled garments before laundering. *Do not* soak wool, spandex, silk or fabrics that are not colourfast.

Mark the Spot

Use a brightly coloured peg to mark the stain, or use a rubber band and wrap it around the area that needs to be spotted prior to laundering. Have family members do this *before* they put their clothes into the linen basket. This will make spots and stains easier to locate and easier to treat. Spots will be obvious, so you don't need to examine each article as you sort.

Now You're Ready to Wash!

Add detergent to the washing machine as it fills up with water. If you are using cold water with powdered detergent and you have a problem with the detergent dissolving, mix it with a little hot water before adding it to the machine – or consider switching to a liquid detergent.

• Add additional laundry aids such as bleach, water softener, laundry booster, etc.

• Load the machine, but do not overload. If you stuff too many garments into the machine the clothes will not clean well, and they'll have more wrinkles too.

• Make sure your load is balanced – not all bunched on one side of the agitator – especially if you are washing one large or heavy item, such as a blanket or bath mat.

• Remember: don't leave the house while you're doing laundry.

If you have room in your laundry or cupboard areas, provide several different coloured laundry baskets for family
members to sort dirty clothes as they are removed – a basket
for whites, colours, jeans (if your family wears a lot of them)
and delicates. You'll be off to a good start and the whole
laundry sorting boogie will go faster. Use these baskets after
washing to hold clothes that need to be folded and to carry
clothes that can be put away.

16

Know When to Hold 'Em, Know When to Fold 'Em

Normally I don't like to use the f-word . . . but not everything can be hung on a hanger. There are some things that simply must be *folded*. Don't worry, though. You don't have to be the empress of elbow grease to quickly fold clothes and put them away.

It's best to hang items that wrinkle easily, such as cotton, rayon, etc. Blouses, dress shirts and dresses that are not knit are best on a hanger. Knits are best folded.

Consider the space your clothes have to fit into before you fold them.

If, for example, drawer space is at a premium in your

house, consider rolling things such as underwear, T-shirts, socks, towels, etc. You can fit more into a drawer or cupboard that way, and wrinkles will be minimal. Rolled clothes also save lots of room in your suitcase – an added bonus for frequent travellers.

Sweaters and sweatshirts are best folded, and you will never have shoulder dimples, either. To fold, lay the garment facedown and fold each side to meet in the middle at the back. This will avoid a line running down the centre of your garment. Fold the sleeves down the back of the garment, then fold the garment in half lengthways. These items can also be rolled effectively.

Socks can be rolled toe to top. You might also want to consider investing in draw dividers made specifically for socks and hose. You will never find your socks in a tangled mess, or worse still, missing. Colours will be obvious and easy to pick out.

And by the way, just to set the record straight, washing machines and dryers positively *do not* eat socks. Nor is there a sock monster in your utility room who steals one sock! Missing socks can sometimes be found wedged between the drum and the machine. Check your trouser legs and shirt sleeves, and check the dryer hose, too. I once found a lonely sock on the driveway – it had tried to escape by shimmying out the dryer hose and up through the vent!

Fitted sheets *can* be tamed. Fold them in half lengthways, then fold each curved end into the middle. Now you have a square end to work with. Fold in half again and then either roll or continue to fold to the size that best fits your storage area. If you don't mind the same sheets on the bed each week, wash them, dry them and put them back on straightaway and you will *never* have to fold them again!

Fold rubber or latex-backed rugs with the fabric side in to prevent the backing from sticking together during storage.

Consider using hooks on the back of the cupboard doors for robes and nightclothes. Don't use suction hooks, though. They're not strong enough to hold clothes.

If doing underwear for multiple family members together, consider buying different brands for each person to make sorting and folding go faster. Try this with socks too.

Keeping a spring-type curtain rod or shower rod set up in the laundry room (if you have one) makes it easy to hang clothes as you remove them from the dryer. Let each person come and claim their own hanging clothes and basket of ready-to-fold or folded clothes. This will cut your laundry time way down. A quick reminder: if the kids have to fold their own clothes, don't let them defeat your system and dress out of the laundry basket all week instead of folding and putting away their things. Otherwise, they will throw the dirty clothes on the floor all week!

Good laundry habits are easy to learn, especially when they become routine.

17

Taking the Dread Out of Dry Cleaning

Not everything we wear can be laundered, and that means a trip to the dry cleaner and the dreaded game of 'will that spot come out?' Most people end up at the dry cleaner because they have clothing stains they can't get out themselves. Luckily for us, professional dry cleaners, with their special solvents, equipment and training, can remove some of the most disastrous-looking stains fairly simply. Successful stain removal depends on three things: the nature of the stain; the type of fabric; and the colourfastness of the dye. Remember to check your care labels. Not all fabrics and dyes are made to withstand the use of cleaning or stain removal agents.

Invisible stains: Many stains that are caused by food, oily substances or beverages may become invisible when they dry. Later on, with exposure to heat or the passage of time, a yellowish or brownish stain will appear. You have probably seen this on clothes you have hung away and pulled out months later. This is caused by the oxidation of the sugar in the staining substance. It is the same thing that makes an apple turn brown once it is peeled and exposed to the air.

You can be a better dry-cleaning customer and help your dry cleaner do a better job for you by pointing out such stains when you take a garment in to be cleaned. The cleaner often treats these stains prior to cleaning, much as you prespot your laundry at home. This pretreatment is vital since the heat of drying or finishing may set the stain, making it impossible to remove.

When an oily substance is exposed to heat or ages in a piece of clothing for a long period of time, it oxidizes. This type of stain can be recognized by its irregular shape on the fabric. Oily stains can be removed easily during the dry-cleaning process provided they have not been there for an extended period of time. Once they are yellow or brown, they are almost impossible to remove.

Perspiration stains: Perspiration can also cause problem stains, especially on silk and wool clothes. Perspiration left in a silk garment can eventually cause deterioration of the fibres.

Repeated exposure to perspiration and body oils can leave clothing with a permanent yellow discoloration and even an offensive odour. Perspiration can react with the dye in the fabric, making it even more difficult to remove the stain.

If you perspire heavily, have your clothes cleaned more frequently, especially in the warmer months.

Important Reminders

Make sure that you point out any unusual care instructions to your cleaner, and make sure that you point out spots and spills, identifying them wherever possible.

• Whether you are doing the cleaning yourself or a professional is doing it, treatment of spots and spills with the right spotter is essential.

• If you remove the care tag, it's a good idea to label it clearly – that is, identify the garment to which it belongs – and pin it to a corkboard in your laundry room or kitchen for future reference.

Now the part we never want to hear – the dry cleaner's responsibility. Dry cleaners are responsible for attempting to remove stains in accordance with professional practice. Sadly, not all stains can be removed, despite the dry cleaner's best efforts.

The more information you give to your dry cleaner and the sooner a garment is brought in, the greater the chance of success in stain removal.

The Dirt on Home Dry-Cleaning Kits

Y̶ou've seen them – those home dry-cleaning kits available in all the stores. What are they good for? Well, if you expect to open the dry-cleaning bag and find clean, sharply pressed clothes straight from the dryer, you'll be disappointed. If, however, you want to extend the time between professional dry cleanings, these kits may be for you.

I have found home dry-cleaning kits to be effective on items such as sweaters, cut velvet, velvet, dry-clean-only blouses – and those garments that are delicate and hard to hand wash and lay flat to dry. They are also great for freshening small blankets, bedspreads, duvets and curtains. Do not force a large bedspread or blanket into the bag. It will be filled with wrinkles when you remove it.

Home dry-cleaning kits do work on suits, although you'll give up the sharply pressed finish. (You may even find occasional spotting on the suit's lining.)

All of these kits come with treated cloths and reusable dryer-safe bags. Some come with separate spotting solution and spotting blotters. They all work relatively the same way:

First, you spot the garment, either with the same sheet that you toss in the bag during the cleaning process, or with a separate spotting liquid. Spotting the garment well is important because, as we all know by now, heat can set stains. Take your time with the spotting procedure and look over the garment well.

Two good home dry-cleaning kits are Persil Revive for use in the dryer and Globright which deoderises and also treats everyday stains including chocolate, tea, coffee, grease and wine.

Carefully follow the directions on the kit you have selected. Do not overcrowd the dryer bag or your clothes will be very wrinkled and require a lot of work with the iron – and that defeats the purpose.

Special Hints from the Palace

• Remove the clothes from the dryer bag immediately, and hang or fold them – whichever is appropriate. Some pressing may be required, depending on the type of fabric.

• Do not use any bag other than that which is provided in the kit, and do not use any additional cleaning chemicals.

• If you don't like the odour of perfume fresheners, check out each kit individually and try several. Some have more perfume than others.

• Again, follow the directions closely.

Are these kits worth the money? Ultimately, that's up to you to decide. If you have a lot of things you want to freshen between cleanings, and if that crisp, pressed look is not vital to you, then yes, give them a try. If, however, your wardrobe consists mostly of business suits and crisply creased trousers, you will probably be disappointed. Will these kits replace your regular trips to the dry cleaner? I don't think so. And I don't think they were intended to.

19
Final Thoughts on Dry Cleaning

I am frequently asked about dry cleaning items such as curtains, bedspreads, duvets, covers on upholstered cushions, slipcovers and antique items. Here are some final thoughts.

Curtains: Dry cleaning or professional laundering can prolong the life of your curtains. With proper care, curtains can be expected to last a long time. Unfortunately, environmental conditions such as humidity, exposure to sunlight and water damage from rain and condensation can discolour and weaken fabric, leaving curtains vulnerable to shredding when they are agitated during the cleaning process. Age, moisture, light, heat and nicotine can also damage curtains and turn them yellow.

Shrinkage is a big concern for curtains that have not been preshrunk, especially cottons and rayons. Your dry cleaner has stretchers to help eliminate this problem.

Distortion and fabric stiffening can also occur during the cleaning process. This depends on the fibre, weave and design of your drapes. In addition, some curtains have a reflective coating that may not make it through the dry-cleaning process.

Talk with your dry cleaner *before* you have your curtains cleaned. Examine them together. Be clear in your expectations and be honest as to the age of your drapes. Otherwise . . . it's curtains!

Bedspreads and duvets: Many bedspreads and duvets should be dry-cleaned or professionally laundered. Check for care instructions at the time of purchase so you know what is recommended. Tailored and quilted pieces are best done professionally.

Be sure to include all matching pieces when you have the bedspread or duvet cleaned. That way colours will remain uniform.

Upholstery and slipcovers: Upholstery is usually cleaned in place by professional cleaners, such as those who do carpet cleaning. These professionals will be able to maintain the colour of your upholstery so that it matches the rest of your furniture.

So, why do cushion covers have zips if we can't take them

off and dry clean or launder them? It is to allow for foam replacement, *not home cleaning*. Once you remove these covers, it is almost impossible to put them back on evenly with the seams straight. My best advice? Never remove and launder cushion covers.

If slipcovers are removed for dry cleaning or laundering, you need to be aware of whether they were preshrunk and what the shrinkage factor is. Check at the time of purchase.

It's a good idea to have slipcovers cleaned by professionals. They can ensure that the proper size machine is used and that there is no crowding, which can set in wrinkles. They also have the right equipment for touch-up pressing.

Antique fabrics: These are your treasures. They belonged to mum or grandmother or a favourite aunt. You love them, you treasure them and now they are dirty.

Antique quilts, linens and fabrics require great care during the cleaning process. Not every cleaner is equipped for this so you may have to check around. Let your cleaner know right away that the item is very old and treasured. Proper cleaning by a careful professional might just well restore an aged and discoloured piece.

Word of mouth is the best way to find a good quality dry cleaner. Don't be afraid to ask around. Ask, too, what the cleaner's policy is on damaged items.

Prolong the Life of Your Fabrics

• Bear in mind that closely woven fabric is more durable than loosely woven fabric.

• Consider sun exposure when selecting fabrics. If you are putting curtains at a sunny window, look at acrylic, polyester and glass fibres.

• Read all the care instructions immediately. If you don't want to be bothered with a lot of care, select another item.

• Rotate curtains at windows that are the same size to vary exposure to light.

• Be sure your cleaner knows what your care label recommends.

• Regular cleaning can prolong the life of all fabrics. Clean your household items on a regular schedule.

20

Ironing and Ironing Boards: Taking the Heat

Nobody likes to iron, but occasionally, no matter how carefully you launder and dry your clothes, you're going to have to iron them too. Ironing can be a nasty chore, but I have some ways to make it easier. Just think of me as Chairman of the Ironing Board!

First of all, if you have to iron, do it in a place you enjoy. Set up the ironing board in the family room or somewhere you can watch television as you work, or near the stereo where you can listen to some music or a book on tape. You might even like to set it up in a room where the family is gathered so that they can all visit you as you work. You can also enlist family members to hang up and put away their clothes as you iron them. (And don't assume I'm talking to mum. Dad should be able to do the ironing just as well!)

Now to the basics.

Cleaning Your Iron

Irons without nonstick finishes: If the iron has a silver sole plate (the metal will be shiny), that usually means it does not have a 'nonstick' finish. To clean these irons, heat the iron to hot on the nonsteam setting, and run it over table salt sprinkled on brown paper. You can remove residue by using white, nongel toothpaste on a damp, soft cloth. Rinse well.

For really heavy buildup, or where fabric has burned to the bottom of a cold iron: protect the body of the iron by covering it with aluminum foil, then spray the sole plate with oven cleaner. Wait 10 minutes, rinse, and clean out the holes on the bottom of the iron with pipe cleaners or cotton buds.

Rinse the bottom well and then, using steam, iron over an old towel or rag before using the iron on clothes.

Irons with nonstick finishes: Clean the sole plate using your favourite laundry prewash on a damp, soft cloth. Do this on a cool iron. Again, iron with steam over an old cloth before ironing clothes.

Cleaning the steam part of the iron: Fill the steam iron with equal portions of white vinegar and water. Let it steam for several minutes, then disconnect the iron and let it sit for one hour. Empty and rinse with clear water and iron over an old cloth, using steam.

Make the Most of Your Time at the Board

For energy-efficient ironing: Put aluminium foil between the ironing board and the cover – shiny side up. The foil will reflect the heat upwards on to the garments you are ironing, so less effort is required by you!

To keep ironing boards clean longer: Spray the cover with spray starch and iron over it.

Ironing delicate fabrics: The secret to ironing these fabrics is to lay a 'press cloth' over them and iron on that. Any old piece of lightweight cotton will work fine. Never lay a bare iron on delicate fabrics.

Collars: Iron both sides of the collar for a crisp, smooth finish. Start at the point and iron inwards to the centre to avoid pushing creases to the tip.

Seams and hems: To avoid creating a line over seams and hems, iron the garment inside out and stop just short of the seam or hemline.

Embroidery: Lay the piece of embroidery face down on a towel, and iron on the reverse side. That way you won't flatten the embroidery.

Large items: Before you start ironing, turn the ironing board around so that you are using the wide end rather than the point. You can cover more area as you iron this way. Fold items such as large tablecloths in half and iron one side, then fold in half again and iron the other two sides.

Dampening clothes: Our mums use to sprinkle clothes with water to help release the wrinkles and make ironing easier. This is still a good idea – especially with all the natural fibres we are wearing. Items that are too dry are very difficult to iron, so use a spray bottle to mist clothes that have dried. If clothes are heavily wrinkled, lay a damp towel on the ironing board and iron – with steam – over it. This works remarkably well on heavy trousers, jeans, etc.

The shoulder pad challenge: Try not to iron over shoulder pads or they will leave an ugly ring on the fabric. Just an additional note: before you launder shoulder pads, tack the filling and the cover of the shoulder pad together so that it will not shift during the laundry and ironing process.

Steaming Strategies

• Test the iron first. If it sticks, jerks or leaves a film on the ironing board cover, then stop – the iron needs to be cleaned before you iron clothes.

• Don't iron over zips, buttons or any lumps.

• Don't iron rubber, suede, leather or stretch-type fabric.

• Don't iron dirty clothes or clothes that you have perspired in. It will set stains and damage the fibres.

• Use only a cool iron on synthetic fibres.

• When in doubt, start with a cool/warm iron.

• Test iron in an inconspicuous area. If in doubt, use a press cloth to avoid 'shine' on the fabric surface.

• Always empty the water from the steam iron when you are done using it to prevent mineral buildup in the water reservoir.

Right Side, Wrong Side, Which Side?

• Iron cotton, net or silky rayon right side up. These fabrics tend to wrinkle more than others, and ironing them on the *wrong* side will not get all the wrinkles out.

• Iron polyester on either side.

• Iron other garments on the wrong side of the fabric for best results. You'll avoid scorching, shine spots and other fabric damage.

Yikes! The Iron Was Too Hot! It's Scorched!

Try soaking the fabric in cold water overnight. That may remove the scorch mark.

On white fabrics, try saturating a cloth with 3 per cent hydrogen peroxide, lay it over the scorch, and iron over it until the mark is removed. *Do not* use this method on coloured fabric.

Refer to the Spot and Stain Removal Guide for more ways to treat scorch marks.

Part II
....
PALACE
PREDICAMENTS

21
Work Clothes

Dirty, greasy work clothes should never be washed with other clothes. Soil may transfer to the other clothes.

Prespotting stains is essential. Treat spots with a good spotter or Spot Shot Instant Carpet Stain Remover®. It's very effective on grease and oil. Launder in the hottest water you can for the fabric type, using a long wash cycle and adding 115 g soda crystals along with your detergent.

If grease and oil are a major problem, spray the areas with WD-40 Lubricant® and wait 10 minutes. Work in undiluted washing-up liquid and launder as usual.

If dust and mud are a concern, prewash the clothes with the hottest possible water and 115 g soda crystals and 115 g laundry borax. After the cycle is complete, add laundry detergent and launder as usual.

For heavily soiled, greasy work clothes, try pouring a can of Coke® in the washing machine with your detergent and launder as usual. The combination of cola syrup and sugar works like magic!

Good water and detergent circulation is important, so don't overcrowd the clothes in the washing machine.

22

Perspiration Stains: They're the Pits!

Perspiration will weaken fabrics, so treat vulnerable areas with care.

The best time to treat those invisible perspiration problems is right after you wear a garment for the first time, *before* you toss it in the washer.

Moisten the underarm area – or any other spot where perspiration stains are a problem – and work in a lather of Fairy soap. Once you've worked up a good lather, toss the garment in the machine and launder as usual.

Working Ace 'wash booster' into the stained fabric is also effective. Just make sure to wet the offending area first!

Always treat perspiration areas on a garment *prior to*

laundering. If odour is present, apply warm water to the area and work in laundry borax. Let sit 30 minutes or so, then launder.

ODORZOUT™ (see page 48) is also an extremely effective odour eliminator. Use it dry on those smelly areas. You can leave it on overnight – you can even put some in your linen basket.

If you already have stains, try dampening the fabric with warm water and working in laundry detergent and Ace. Let that soak about 30 minutes and launder as usual.

I have found that soaking garments (whites or colours) in Brilliant Bleach™ from Soapworks (see page 32) is very effective for removing underarm stains.

You can also try to clean existing stains with heated white vinegar. Spray it on the fabric and then work in laundry borax. This works well on odour as well as stains.

If the fabric has changed colour, try spraying with sudsy ammonia, let sit about 15 minutes, then launder as usual.

Bear in mind that yellowed or discoloured fabric may be damaged. The garment may not be salvageable.

Treat everything prior to washing for the first time and do try switching brands of antiperspirant. Never wear shirts or blouses more than one day if you have a perspiration problem. You may find that wearing natural fibres such as cottons will be less of a problem than polyester and polyester blends. If your problem is serious you may want to try underarm shields. They trap moisture before it can reach the fabric. They can be removed and thrown away each day, and can't be seen through the garment. Look for them in lingerie stores.

23

Socks and Panty Hose

*F*olklore: *if the legs of stockings, panty hose, leggings or socks intertwine on a clothesline or in a dryer, the owner of the garment is assured of joy and happiness.*

Socks

White socks: To get white socks really clean, soak them for an hour in 3.8 litres hot water and 2 tablespoons dishwasher detergent. Pour the socks and soaking solution into the washing machine and launder as usual and they'll be clean and bright like you've never imagined.

You can also whiten socks by soaking in hot water to which you have added the slices of 1 lemon or 100 ml lemon juice. Soak several hours or overnight. Put the socks in the washing machine and launder as usual.

Foot odour: Turn your socks into sweet-smelling odour beaters by adding 25 g bicarbonate of soda to 3.8 litres water. Spin the socks in the washing machine without rinsing out the soda solution. Dry as usual.

To increase the life of your panty hose: Dip them in water, wring them out, put them in a plastic bag and freeze them solid. When you remove them from the freezer, let them thaw and dry completely. They'll be ready to wear and they'll last longer! Do this before you wear them for the first time.

To increase the elasticity in panty hose: Add 2 tablespoons of white vinegar to the rinse water.

To wash panty hose with ease in the washing machine: Use an old panty hose leg to hold a pair of good panty hose. Just knot the end of the panty hose leg at the top so the panty hose won't come out during washing. Adding some fabric softener to the rinse will lubricate the fibres and make the hose last longer and cut down on electricity. Out of softener? Use some hair conditioner!

Buy two, get one free: If you are down to your last pairs of panty hose and they all have runs in one leg, take two pairs of panty hose, cut off the damaged legs, and combine the two remaining 'half pairs' to make one good pair! And if they happen to be control top, you've got double the tummy control!

24
Getting in the Swim

Swimwear is expensive, but correct care, washing and storage will ensure a long life.

Always read the care label before buying swimwear. This way you will be prepared for whatever care is required.

After swimming in a chlorinated pool, soak your suit for 15 minutes or so in cold water with a little liquid fabric softener. Rinse in cold water, then wash in cool water with mild detergent. Rinse well again and dry in the shade. Chlorine is very hard on fabrics, weakening them and changing the colour, so be sure to rinse the suit as soon as you can. Never put your suit away without rinsing it out first.

If the suit has been worn in seawater, soak it for a few minutes in cold water to remove the salt, then wash in cold water with mild detergent. Rinse well and dry in the shade.

Fold the suit in shape once it's dry. Store in tissue or in a perforated plastic bag for winter. (A perforated bag will allow the fabric to breathe.)

25

Hats and Handbags

You can't toss these in the washing machine. But you can still clean them.

Leather bags: Clean these quite easily with a cloth that you have wrung out in warm water and lathered with a bar of moisturizing face soap, such as Dove®. Rub well, rinsing the cloth as needed and working the soap in until all dirt has been removed. Buff well with a soft cloth.

You may also polish the bag with leather cream or polish, following the directions on the container. Laying the bag in the sun for 15 minutes or so will allow the polish to absorb better.

Never store leather bags in plastic. Wrap in cloth or tissue. Never store leather and plastic or vinyl bags together. The leather will bleed colour on to the other bags, ruining them.

Patent leather bags: Use a little petroleum jelly on a soft cloth to buff these to a brilliant shine. Buff once more with a clean, dry cloth.

Plastic or vinyl bags: These bags should be washed with a soft cloth or sponge and a mild soap or all-purpose cleaner. Rinse well and buff. If you want to restore the shine, apply a little spray furniture polish to a soft cloth and buff.

Suede bags: Brush suede bags frequently using a suede brush. Grease marks can be removed with a little dry-cleaning fluid or try a little undiluted white vinegar on a soft cloth. Brush the nap into position and allow to dry out of the sun, then brush again.

If the nap is severely flattened, steam the bag lightly over a pan of boiling water. Do not allow the bag to become too wet. Air-dry and then brush well.

Evening bags: Clean these gently with a soft cloth and some dry-cleaning fluid. Dry well by blotting or using the hair-dryer. Beaded bags can be lightly dusted with talcum powder to absorb dirt. Enclose the bag in a towel, wait 24 hours and then gently brush. Take care to not loosen threads holding the beads.

Heads Up

Caps: Clean soiled baseball caps the easy way by putting them in the dishwasher on the top rack. Run through the entire cycle, take out and allow to air dry. Washed this way, they will retain their shape. Works well for crowns too!

Hats that are not washable can be cleaned by using a soot-and-dirt removal sponge, available at hardware stores. Rub the dry sponge over the soiled areas of the hat, as if you were erasing with a large eraser. Do this outside or over a rubbish bin or sink. Continue to work until you have removed all the soiling you possibly can. This is effective for felt and cowboy-style hats, too.

Cool water and shampoo work well on nylon or knit caps. Add a few drops of hair conditioner to rinse water to soften and condition the fibres. My Canadian friends will be pleased to know that this method works well on toques!

26

Ties: Don't Let Them Tie You in Knots

Ties are generally not washable, which is a shame because nothing gets more food spills and dipped into more things than ties. This does not mean that you can't successfully spot clean them, though.

If you have a tie with a food or beverage spill, first slip a pad of paper towelling in the opening between the front and the back of the tie. This will prevent the spot from forcing its way through the tie. Use Dylon Stain Remover 3 which comes with its own applicator to remove stains without leaving rings. Read the instructions carefully.

When ironing a tie, lay it flat on the ironing board and

cover with a press cloth (a lightweight towel will work) and press it with steam. Hang to dry completely. When storing ties, hang them or roll them (great for travel) to prevent wrinkles and creases.

㉗
Snap, Zip and Hook! (No, It's Not a New Breakfast Cereal!)

The best advice I can give you is zip your zips, snap your snaps, hook your hooks and button your buttons.

If you don't, you run the risk of catching, pulling or tearing fabric, damaging the interlocking mechanism (zip) and pulling the buttons off during the washing process.

Just Zip It!

If you have a zip that sticks and doesn't want to pull up, rub it with a little soap, paraffin or candle wax. This will lubricate the teeth and get it moving.

If your zip on trousers, skirts, etc., doesn't want to stay up, add a button, snap or some Velcro just above it.

To give your zip a little extra 'stick', spritz it with hair spray. That will help it stay zipped.

Button Bonus

To keep buttons from falling off, dab a little clear nail polish on the thread in the centre of the button. This will keep the thread from wearing through so easily.

For buttons that get hard wear, stitch them on with dental floss. It may not be as pleasing to the eye as thread, but the buttons won't fall off!

28
Beads and Sequins: Let's Face the Music and Dance

Laundering: Some sequined and beaded clothes can be washed. Here's how to keep them looking great:

• Button them completely prior to laundering.

• Turn clothes inside out prior to laundering.

• If machine washable, use only the gentle cycle set for approximately 2 or 3 minutes, with cold water and mild detergent.

• If the item is hand washable, use mild laundry soap or a little shampoo and cold water.

• Put a little hair conditioner in the final rinse if the garment is knitted.

• Always hang to dry or lay flat – never dry in the dryer.

Freshening: Spritz lightly with undiluted vodka under the arms and around the neck and cuffs. Hang to dry.

Spills: Many beaded outfits are labelled 'spot clean only'. Use a little soda water or Dylon Stain Remover 3. Apply any moisture sparingly and then use a hair-dryer to dry the spot quickly to avoid a moisture ring.

29
Furs:
Real and Synthetic

If you have a fur coat, you know who you are, so no lectures.

Any fur garment that is worn regularly should be cleaned regularly too. This means once a year by a professional cleaner who specializes in fur. Best to have your fur cleaned just prior to storing it for the summer – this also applies to synthetic furs. A professional cleaner will remove stains, such as makeup, food and beverages that can ruin fur. Keeping it clean will also deter moths.

It's a good idea to wear a soft scarf around the neck to keep stains and body oil away from a fur collar.

Hang furs and synthetic furs on well-padded hangers in a cloth bag. Don't use plastic. Shake the fur well when you take it from storage. You'll want to air it prior to wearing as well.

㉚
Table Linens

Nothing makes a table look better than a beautiful table-cloth and napkins – but cleaning up after the meal can be a bit of a chore. Here are some foolproof ways to make the cleanup fast and easy.

Stain-proofing tablecloths: Spraying tablecloths with Scotchgard® Fabric Protector or a similar product prior to using will allow spills to wash out. Don't spray the cloth on top of a wood table. You'll spoil the finish.

Removing Stains from Tablecloths

Bleach white cotton and linen items. Soak coloured items in heavy-duty detergent solution.

For white linens, you can also dissolve 2 denture-cleaning tablets in warm water. Spread out the stained area in a bath-tub or sink. Pour on the solution and let soak for 30 minutes, then launder as usual.

Soaking stained table linens in Brilliant Bleach™ (see page 32) produces beautiful results. Soak until the stain is removed – even several days – without harming the fabric.

Removing red wine stains: These methods will work on any type of red stain, including red pop, cranberry juice and fruit punches:

Always keep some white wine handy for red wine spills. Pour the white wine on the red wine and it will remove the stain. Do this as soon as you can.

Keep soda water on hand for red stains too. Pour the soda through the stain, preferably over the sink. Pretreat and launder as usual.

Removing dried tea and black coffee stains: For tea stains, drape the stained item over a bowl or sink. Sprinkle with laundry borax until the entire stain is covered. Pour a kettle full of hot water around the stain, working toward the centre. Repeat if necessary and then launder
as usual. For dried coffee stains, treat with a solution of 50 per cent glycerin and 50 per cent warm water. Rinse and blot well. Treat with laundry presoak prior to laun-dering.

Stains on cloth napkins: The most common stain on cloth

napkins is lipstick. To remove this, spray the area with WD-40 Lubricant®, wait 10 minutes, then work in undiluted washing-up liquid and launder as usual.

For food and beverage stains, treat with a commercial prespotter or one of the ones we made in Chapter 5, or use Spot Shot Instant Carpet Stain Remover®. Be sure not to let the spotters dry on the napkins before laundering.

You can also soak both white and coloured napkins in Brilliant Bleach™ (see page 32) without damaging the fabrics or colours.

Storing Tablecloths Wrinkle-Free

Instead of folding tablecloths, fold minimally lengthways and then roll the cloth. It takes less room to store and will not wrinkle as easily, either. Hang cloths that wrinkle easily over a hanger covered with a fabric cover. A towel works well.

SPECIAL TIP ....

Never starch tablecloths before storing or they will yellow. If hanging, cover with a sheet or cloth. Don't use plastic as this too will cause yellowing.

Caring for Plastic and Vinyl Tablecloths

Clean plastic and vinyl tablecloths by wiping with a clean damp cloth and rinsing well. For stubborn stains, make a paste of lemon juice and cream of tartar and work it into the stain. Allow the paste to sit on the stain for a few minutes, then rinse. Let dry before folding.

Sprinkling clean plastic tablecloths with a little talcum powder before storing them will prevent stickiness and mildew.

31
Let the Light Shine: Cleaning Lampshades

*F*abric covered and stitched: I find the easiest way to wash these shades is in the bathtub! Put enough cool water in the tub to allow you to roll the shade on its side. Add some mild soap or detergent. Swirl the shade in the water/soap combination gently. Remove the soapy water and rinse the shade, using the same method – make sure the water is cool. Shake the shade gently to remove excess water and allow to dry in an upright position. Drying can be speeded up by using the hair-dryer. This works particularly well on thick and corded areas that dry more slowly.

Paper shades and shades with glue: You can't wet these shades, so your best bet is to vacuum them frequently with the duster brush on your vacuum. You can also purchase a soot-and-dirt removal sponge at the hardware store. It's basically a big block eraser that you use dry to erase the dirt away. It works beautifully, just as long as you don't allow the shade to become heavily soiled. This eraser can also be used on washable shades.

Make sure the soot-and-dirt removal sponge is used dry on a dry object. You may wash the sponge, but be sure to let it dry before using it again.

Act Natural™ microfibre cloths (see their website: www.euronetusa.com) also work well on lampshades. Dampen the cloth (only slightly damp, please) and wipe down the shade. It will remove dirt and hair without harming the shade.

Parchment shades: Dust or vacuum these shades regularly. You can use the soot-and-dirt removal sponge on these too. Even a slice of white bread with the crust removed will work! Rub the bread over the shade, preferably on the outside, and watch the dirt fall away with the crumbs.

Plastic shades: Wash these in warm water and mild soap. Dry them well and then restore the shine with spray furniture polish.

Scorch marks: Unfortunately, scorch marks on lampshades are not removable. The material is weakened by the heat and the damage is permanent. Take care when choosing bulbs. Scorch marks are generally caused by bulbs that are too large for the shade.

㉜
Slipcovers

Some slipcovers can be laundered in the washing machine. Just make sure to wash unusually large or bulky covers in a large, commercial washing machine.

Don't forget to test for colourfastness (see Chapter 12). Shake out or vacuum the slipcovers before washing and remember to follow the instructions on the care label.

Pretreat any spots or spills before laundering. Fairy soap worked into the arms and headrest will remove a lot of the greasy soiling. Wash in cool water and mild detergent and make sure to rinse well – twice if necessary. Do not overcrowd the slipcovers in the machine or you will be disappointed with the results.

Dry according to the care label. Heavy items such as these need room to breathe, so if you're going to hang your slipcovers to dry, make sure to spread them over several lines, spaced at least 30 cm apart. If you're using the dryer you should check and rearrange the covers frequently.

Press slipcovers with an iron heated to the appropriate temperature for the fabric type, and fit the covers back on the furniture while they are still slightly damp. Not only will they stretch more readily when damp, but they will shrink slightly as they dry, and that will draw out wrinkles and creases. When the covers are good and dry you may want to apply a light coating of fabric protector to help keep them soil-resistant.

33

Don't Throw in the Towel!

It's lovely to step out of the shower and wrap yourself in a clean, fluffy towel – what I call a *warm fuzzy*. Towels are pretty low maintenance; nevertheless there are some things you can do to keep them at their best. Read on . . . what follows is absorbing!

Washing towels in hot water with your favourite laundry detergent or soap will remove normal soiling. Add 115 g soda crystals to a full load of towels if you want to kick your detergent up a notch and clean more effectively.

Presoaking heavily soiled towels is always a good idea. Soak them in hot water and 55 g laundry borax, and you will deodorize them as well!

Fabric softener will provide you with soft, fluffy towels, but overuse will make the towels less absorbent. Use softener every second or third time instead of every time you launder them. You can also use 100 ml white vinegar as a softening agent. And no, the towels will not smell like vinegar!

Dark-dyed towels will lose a considerable amount of dye during their first several washings. If you have faded towels the same colour as the new ones, wash them together to restore some of the colour to the old batch. Adding 140 g table salt to the wash water the first time you launder dark towels will keep them from fading as quickly.

Do not wash dark towels and light towels together, ever! The light towels will pick up the colour and fuzz from the dark ones, and the dark towels will end up with light-coloured lint all over them.

Always wash new towels prior to using to make them more absorbent. If you find yourself with towels that are slick and will not absorb, here's what to do.

• Soak them in cold water and 35 g Epsom salts overnight. Then place in the washing machine with your favourite detergent and launder as usual.

• Wash nonabsorbent towels several times in a row and do not add fabric softener.

• Sometimes hanging these towels to dry instead of drying in the dryer for a couple of washings works well.

Do not wash anything else with towels. Washing things together transfers lint from item to item. Always wash towels in the hottest possible water.

If your towels have a mildew odour, sprinkle them lightly with ODORZOUT™ (see page 48) and let sit for a day or so, then dump into the washing machine (towels and ODOR-ZOUT™) and launder as usual.

③④
Window Treatments

Be sure to read the care label and closely follow instructions when you are cleaning your drapes and curtains. Never try to wash curtains that should be dry-cleaned.

You can extend the life of window coverings by vacuuming them frequently with the upholstery attachments on your vacuum cleaner. You may also take them down and shake them, or tumble them in the dryer on the air setting.

Do not allow curtains to become heavily soiled before cleaning, especially if they are labeled 'dry clean only'.

Dry cleaning does not clean as well as wet cleaning, and all soil may not be removed.

Sunlight weakens and damages fibre and colour. If the curtains or drapes are covering a particularly sunny window, hanging a blind or shade to protect the fabric might be a wise idea.

Remove all hooks, etc., from curtains prior to washing. Follow the directions for the type of fabric on the care label directions.

Some curtains can be dried in the dryer. Check the care label. Just be sure not to overcrowd the dryer, and remember to rearrange them often during the drying cycle.

If pressing is required, remove the curtains while damp and iron. This will make it easier to remove the wrinkles. For a crisp finish, use starch or ironing spray. Remember, two light sprays are better than one heavy one and will prevent white 'flaking' on the fabric.

Sizing and starch will help to repel dirt as well.

If you've washed sheer or lace-type curtains, pressing them gently while damp and hanging them slightly damp will encourage them to fall into gentle folds at the window.

Plastic shower curtains: Wash these in the washing machine with several old, light-coloured towels. Add 350 ml white vinegar and your normal detergent, fill with warm water, and use the gentle cycle. Remove the curtain promptly from the machine and hang immediately. This method will remove soap scum and dirt. If mould and mildew are a problem, use 350 ml liquid chlorine (household) bleach instead of white vinegar and follow the above directions.

㉟
Bedtime

We're going to wash those pillows, sheets, blankets and duvets. No sleeping on the job!

Pillows

To freshen pillows, tumble them in the clothes dryer set on air or warm for 30 minutes with several barely damp light-coloured towels and a dryer fabric softener sheet. Don't use the fabric softener sheet if you have fragrance allergies.

Fibre-filled pillows: These flatten with use, so chances are you'll want to restore their bulk and softness. Clean them in your washing machine every couple of months, and choose a windy day if possible. Wash the pillows in cold or lukewarm water with a mild detergent, and use a short cycle. If you have allergies, try Fresh Breeze Laundry Soap™ by Soapworks (see page 32). Make sure the pillows are rinsed well, then spin them dry.

If you are washing pillows by hand, use cool water and mild suds, and press out all the water you can. Rinse several times to remove all the soap, then press and roll out the water.

Hang pillows to dry in a shady, breezy location if possible, turning them frequently. Finally, place pillows in the dryer on the lowest setting to fluff the filling. Adding a new tennis ball or clean tennis shoe in the dryer will help to pump up the volume!

Place pillows inside zipped pillow covers to keep them clean and fresh longer.

Feather pillows: Wash these in cool suds and dry them in the shade. Heat can release traces of oil in the feathers and cause them to give off unpleasant odours.

Make sure you allow plenty of time for the feathers to dry. Fluff and shake the pillow frequently to rearrange the feathers for better drying.

You may put feather pillows in the dryer on the air setting to reposition the feathers and add bounce to the pillows. Again, putting in a couple of tennis balls or clean tennis shoes will beat the feathers up and add fluff. Keeping feather pillows in zipped pillow protectors is also a good idea.

Other pillows: There are a lot of different pillows on the market these days, including specially formed cervical pillows. Wash them according to the care label so you don't damage the filling.

Sheets

Always wash sheets before using them for the first time.

Mend tears before laundering or they will become huge holes.

Wash dark sheets separately from white or light colours to avoid colour runs.

Use warm water for polyester and blends. Use hot water for 100 per cent cotton sheets. Dry according to care label directions, usually on medium.

Flannel Sheets and Pillowcases

Launder these in the washing machine with warm water, and always make sure to wash them before using for the first time. Bear in mind that flannel sheets have an enormous amount of lint, so they may not be suitable for people with allergies (although the more they are laundered the less severe the lint will be). Rinse with warm water and 250 ml white vinegar to help with the lint problem, and make sure you clean the lint filter frequently during the drying cycle the first few times you wash and dry the sheets. Wash flannel separately from all other fabrics.

Blankets

If the care label indicates that your blankets are machine washable, which most are, make sure the machine has plenty of room for movement between the folds of the blanket. Wash with mild soap in cold water and add 250 ml white vinegar to the final rinse to remove any soap residue and keep the blankets soft. If the care tag indicates, dry in a warm dryer or out of direct sunlight over several clotheslines strung at least 30 cm apart to avoid stretching the blanket. Store blankets well by wrapping them in plastic, or inside a clean pillowcase.

For electric blankets or mattress pads, follow the care label directions carefully to avoid damaging the wiring and creating a possible fire hazard.

Bedspreads

Washable spreads should be laundered according to the care label directions. Nylon, polyester, polyester blends and cotton bedspreads all wash well. Rayons, silks and acetates should be dry-cleaned.

Chenille spreads, which are quite popular again, are easily laundered in the washing machine. Use warm water and mild detergent and rinse well. Dry in the dryer and shake well to restore the nap when you remove chenille from the dryer. Linting, which is common in these types of spreads, will stop after a few washings. Be sure to keep your dryer's lint filter well cleaned when drying these spreads.

For heavily quilted spreads you can use tennis balls or a clean tennis shoe to pump up the volume on the quilting.

Duvets

I find that it's best – and also easiest – to have these cleaned professionally. If you do decide to launder yours, use a commercial-size washing machine, using the shortest possible cycle.

Do not wash these more frequently than you have to. Air the duvet frequently instead, and use a duvet cover that can be laundered as needed.

Feather Beds

Follow the directions that come with your feather bed and accessories. Be sure to read all of the cleaning information and follow care instructions carefully.

Mattresses

It's important to turn your mattress every three months to allow for even wear. Alternate between turning it end to end and side to side.

Covering a mattress with a pad or a plastic zip mattress protector is your best defence against stains, especially on a child's bed. A cloth pad is much cooler than plastic.

If you are faced with cleaning up a wet spill, such as urine, absorb all the moisture you can with paper towels or rags, applying pressure as you blot. Clean the area with Spot Shot Instant Carpet Stain Remover® and stand the mattress on its side against a wall to speed drying and keep moisture from going deeper into the mattress. Once the mattress is dry, apply a layer of ODORZOUT™ (see page 48) to absorb the odour. ODORZOUT™ is an odour eliminator, not a cover-up. If you can lay the mattress out in the sun to dry, it will speed up the process.

36
Preserving Your Wedding Gown

Wedding gowns are expensive investments, but with so much excitement leading up to the big day, cleaning the dress afterwards rarely crosses our minds. Often the dress is quickly discarded in favour of more comfortable travel attire, then it's left to lay while we trip off on our honeymoon. Yet, with just a little bit of care you can preserve the dress, for sentimental reasons perhaps, or for your own daughter to wear someday. Here's what you need to know.

First, don't leave the store without a care label. If a care label is not sewn into the gown, be sure to get written cleaning instructions from the store assistant or seamstress.

Once you have chosen your gown, it's best to leave it at the store until the last possible moment. You'll avoid wrinkling that way. If you bring your dress home prior to the big day, decide where you are going to hang it to avoid wrinkling – perhaps an over-the-door hanger in a spare room. Do not hang your precious dress in the attic or the basement. You'll only be inviting dust, dirt, bugs, dampness and water damage.

Now what about after the wedding? Don't just throw your dress down. Hang it on a padded hanger. Assign some-one to pick up the dress within a day or two after the wed-ding and transport it to the cleaner you have chosen. Those spots and spills and lipstick smudges from all those happy kisses will come out much more easily if you have the dress cleaned sooner, *not* later. Ask your mum, sister, or best friend to help out. Whatever you do, don't come home from your honeymoon to a dirty dress laying in a pile on the floor. Even if it never is worn again, you can have beautiful pillows made from the fabric and veiling to use on a bed. That's what I did!

Always have the dress professionally cleaned *before* you put it into storage. Your dress may have invisible stains from food, beverages, perfume and body oil. If these stains are not properly cleaned, they can become permanent. Try to point out stains or spills to your cleaner *before* cleaning.

A lot of wedding gowns are beaded or lavishly trimmed. Inspect these trims with your cleaner prior to cleaning, since many of them are not made to withstand the dry-cleaning process. Beads, glitter and pearls are made of coated plastic and may be attached to the dress with adhesives that will not weather cleaning chemicals. Some trims may yellow during the process. Some items 'dyed to match' may not be colour-fast and may not match after cleaning.

Look for a qualified, experienced cleaner in your area who will discuss all of these things with you and closely examine your dress for potential problems.

Storing Your Gown

Sadly, no cleaning process or storage method can guarantee against yellowing and deterioration of the fabric in your gown. There are, however, steps that you can take to ensure the best possible results.

• Have your dress packed in a special heirloom storage box. You can have your cleaner pack the dress, or buy the box and pack it yourself. Remember to use non-acid tissue paper.

• Wrap the dress in a sheet if it is not boxed. Do not store in plastic or it will yellow.

• Stuff the bodice and sleeves with white, non-acid tissue paper to prevent permanent wrinkles.

• Store headpieces, veils, shoes and other accessories separately. A box or bag will be fine. No plastic, though.

• Store in a cool, dry place. The basement and the attic, though popular, are not good choices.

• If you decide to store your dress on a hanger, hanging it from the sewn-in straps will prevent damage to the shoulders.

• Look your gown over once a year – Valentine's Day is a memorable date – to ensure that no spots have been overlooked. If you find any spotting or discoloration, have the dress treated by a professional cleaner as soon as possible.

Follow these tips and your wedding gown will have a happy future.

37
Cleaning Guide for Fabric Types

I am the 'stain stalker', and in these next pages I am going to walk you through laundry procedures for certain fabric types and unusual items.

Acetate: This is a temperamental fabric. Do not allow it to become heavily soiled and do not use an enzyme detergent when laundering. Acetate is commonly used for curtains, brocades, taffetas and satin. (Think evening wear.) It's also a popular lining. You can machine wash acetate in cold water or you can hand wash. Be sure not to spin or wring acetate as this will set wrinkles. Rinse extremely well and press with a cool (low setting) iron on the wrong side of the fabric.

Acrylic: This fabric should be laundered frequently since it can retain perspiration odours. Acrylic is usually machine washable in cool water. Check the care label. Dry flat or hang to dry, being sure to reshape the garment while it is still damp.

Angora: This wool is made from rabbit fur or goat hair. Angora sheds a lot, although if it's blended with nylon it will shed less. Wash angora in warm or cool water using a very mild soap or a little shampoo. Do not rub, twist or lift the garment up and down in the water as this will cause stretching. Washing in a sink is best. Let the water run out and then press the liquid out of the garment. Rinse well again, pressing the water out. Roll the garment in a towel and then reshape. Dry flat out of the sun. Do not press – instead, hold a steam iron just above the garment to remove wrinkles.

Blends: Blends, such as cotton/polyester, are made from combined fibres. To launder these fabrics, follow the guidelines for the most delicate or the most prominent fibre. The most common blends are cotton/polyester, cotton/linen and silk/polyester.

Brocades: Use care when laundering brocades. You don't want to crush or flatten the pile design. Hand wash in cool water or dry clean according to the care label. Do not wring. Iron on the 'wrong' side using a press cloth or towel between the fabric and the iron.

Canvas: A heavy, firm, very tightly woven fabric, canvas was originally made from cotton or linen, but now it comes in synthetics or blends. Machine wash canvas in cold water and tumble dry on a low setting. Test for colourfastness before washing. If it's not colourfast, have it dry-cleaned.

Cashmere: This is an expensive fibre that comes from the undercoat of cashmere goats. Treat it with respect. Dry clean these prizes or hand wash with care in cool water and well-dissolved gentle soap. Rinse well and do not wring. Dry flat, reshaping the garment as it dries. Iron on the 'wrong' side while still damp with a cool iron, if necessary.

Chiffon: This is a very thin, transparent fabric, made from silk or synthetic fibres. Hand wash as you would silk.

Chintz: Glazed cotton, and often printed. Dry clean this fabric unless the label states that it can be washed. Follow the care label instructions carefully.

Corduroy: Take care when washing corduroy. It wears well, but care is needed to avoid crushing and distorting the pile. Turn corduroy inside out and launder using warm water. Dry at a normal setting. Remove from the dryer while still damp and smooth the seams, pockets, etc. Hang to complete drying, and iron on the 'wrong' side of the fabric. Pile may be restored by brushing gently.

Cotton: This natural vegetable fibre is woven and knitted into fabrics in all weights and textures. Hand wash lightweight fabrics such as organdy and batiste and hang to air dry. Iron when damp with a hot iron.

Machine wash light-coloured and white medium to heavyweight cottons in warm water. Use cold water for bright colours that may bleed. Dry on a low dryer setting. Remove from the dryer while still damp and iron with a hot iron right away.

Damask: This is a jacquard-weave fabric. It may be made of cotton, linen, silk, wool or a blend. Hand wash lightweight fabrics and be sure to check the individual fibre listings. Dry clean silk, wool and all heavier weight fabrics.

Denim: If you have jeans, you know this strong fabric is prone to shrinking, streaking and fading. Machine wash denim in warm water. Blue and other deep colours bleed the first several washings, so be sure to wash separately. Washing older, faded jeans with the new ones will restore some of their original colour. Dry at low settings to avoid shrinkage. Iron while damp if necessary and be aware that jeans may bleed colour on to your ironing board.

Down: Down is the soft underfeather of waterfowl that is often combined with adult feathers. It is machine washable *and* dry-cleanable. Just be sure to follow the care label closely. Much of the treatment will depend on the fabric covering the down, so pay attention to manufacturer's directions.

Do not air-dry down. It dries too slowly and mould or mildew may form in the process. Dry in your dryer, using a large capacity dryer if need be. Set temperatures low (under 60°C/140°F), fluffing and turning the item often. Make sure to dry the item thoroughly. This can take time.

Want really fluffy duvets and pillows? Putting a clean tennis shoe or tennis ball in with the item will fluff it up!

Flannel: Flannel is actually a napped fabric, and it comes in a plain or twill-type weave. Cotton and synthetics should be washed according to the care label, but when in doubt, use cool water and mild detergent. Dry at a low dryer setting and remove flannel while damp to avoid wrinkles. You may also line-dry this fabric. Wool flannel should be dry-cleaned.

Gabardine: Firm, tightly woven twill fabric, often worsted wool, but sometimes made of cotton and synthetic fibres. We are seeing a large amount of synthetic fibres sold as gabardine in trousers and blazers for men and women. Follow your label directions – many synthetics are machine washable and dryable. If the care label says dry clean, be sure to do so.

Lace: An extremely delicate fabric, lace may be made of cotton, linen or synthetic. Wash using a mild soap or detergent intended for delicates. Avoid rubbing since it will distort the fibres. Rinse well without wringing, shape by hand, and hang to air-dry or dry flat. Delicate lace pieces may need to be reshaped and pinned down to dry. If you must iron lace, do so over a terrycloth towel. (White is best.) Never put lace in the dryer.

Leather and suede: Generally, leather and suede are not washable. Check your care label carefully. If you have washable leather items, wash them by hand and be sure to protect them with a leather spray protectant. To clean suede, rub it with another piece of suede or a suede brush (not any other kind of brush) to restore the nap and keep it looking new.

Remember, leather needs to breathe, so do not cover it with plastic or store in a tightly enclosed area. If you are looking for a dust cover for leather or suede, use cloth – an old pillowcase is ideal.

To remove spots from leather (not for suede), try using cuticle remover. Rub it into the spot, wait 10 minutes, and then massage the area with a cloth dipped in the cuticle remover. Wipe down thoroughly.

To remove spots from suede, try dabbing with white vinegar.

Linen: A tough fabric that withstands high temperatures, linen is a favourite in hot climates. It is made of natural flax fibre, and comes in light to heavyweight fabrics. Hand wash or machine wash linen in warm water (again, read your care label). If the fabric is colourfast you may remove stains and brighten the fabric with an oxygen bleach, such as Ace, or Brilliant Bleach™ from Soapworks (see page 32). Do not use chlorine (household) bleach.

Iron while still damp, and to help prevent creasing you may treat with starch or an ironing spray. Press heavyweight linens with a hot iron, and for lighter weight linen and blends (linen, plus other fibres), iron with a warm iron.

Linen is also dry-cleanable.

Mohair: An oldie but a goodie! This is fibre taken from angora goats. Follow the directions for cleaning wool.

Nylon: This is a durable synthetic fibre that comes in varying weights and is often blended with other fibres. When used alone it is machine washable in warm water. It can also be cleaned.

Dry on a low setting or hang to dry using a nonmetal hanger. Do not dry in sunlight – that will cause yellowing. Nonchlorine bleach is best for nylon.

Organdy: Think party dress! Sheer and lightweight, organdy is actually a cotton fibre. Hand wash this and iron damp with a hot iron. Use starch as you iron to give it a crisp look. May also be dry-cleaned.

Polyester: This strong synthetic fibre won't stretch or shrink, which is probably why it's so popular. It comes in various weights and textures, and is often found blended with cotton and wool.

Wash polyester in warm water. Tumble dry and make sure not to let it sit in the dryer, because that will encourage wrinkles. Remove it immediately and you may not need to iron it. If ironing *is* necessary, make sure to use a low setting.

If the polyester is blended with another fibre, just follow the washing instructions for the more delicate fibre.

Ramie: Very similar to linen, ramie is a natural fibre made from – what else – the ramie plant! It can be used alone or blended with other fibres, such as ramie/cotton.

Machine wash in warm water, tumble dry and iron while damp with a hot iron. Avoid twisting the fibres or they will become distorted. May be dry-cleaned also.

Rayon: This is a synthetic fibre that is sometimes called 'viscose'. Follow the care label directions closely, but for the very best results, have this fabric dry-cleaned. Dry-cleaning not only cleans well, but it gives rayon the crisp pressing it needs to maintain its shape and good looks.

Satin: Originally made only from silk, this shiny fabric is available in acetate, cotton, nylon and even polyester.

Dry clean satin made out of silk and acetate. You may wash cotton, nylon and polyester satins, as long as you follow the washing instructions for those fibres.

Seersucker: You've seen this fabric in shirts, blouses and nightwear. It has puckered stripes that are woven in during the manufacturing process. Seersucker is most frequently made of cotton, but it's also available in nylon and polyester. Be guided by the fibre content for washing and drying.

Drip-dry or tumble dry and iron on low heat if necessary.

Silk: This is a natural fibre made by the silkworm. It is a delicate fabric that requires special care to avoid damage.

Check the care labels, but you may be able to hand wash crepe de Chine, thin, lightweight and medium weight silk in lukewarm water with mild soap or detergent. You can also use cold water with cold water detergent.

Do not use chlorine (household) bleach. You may use Brilliant Bleach™ by Soapworks (see page 32) without damaging the fibres.

Rinsing silk well is important. Rinse several times in cold water to remove all suds. Towel blot and dry flat. Do not wring or rub silk.

Iron on the 'wrong' side of the fabric with a warm iron.

If your care label indicates that the garment is machine washable, follow the directions with the utmost care. Dry cleaning works best for suits, pleated silks and silks that are not colourfast.

Do not use strong spotters or enzyme spotters on silk.

Spandex: Spandex is added to other fibres to give them stretch and elasticity. Machine wash in warm water on the delicate or gentle cycle. Do not use chlorine bleach. Do not put them in the dryer, or iron; high heat will break down spandex fibres. Line dry or dry flat, per care label.

If you have exercise clothes containing spandex, be sure to launder each time you wear them. Body oil can break down spandex fibres.

Terrycloth: A towelling-type of fabric, terrycloth has a looped pile made of cotton or cotton/polyester blend. You find it in towels, of course, and even sleepwear.

Machine wash in warm or hot water. Tumble or line dry. Add softener for a softer texture.

Velour: This is a napped fabric that is available in wool, cotton, silk and synthetics. Dry clean unless the care label indicates it can be washed and dried.

Velvet: A beautiful soft pile fabric, velvet comes in silk, rayon or cotton. Dry clean for best results.

To raise the pile on velvet, steam from the 'wrong' side over a pot of boiling water. Hold the fabric at least 30 cm from the water, and be careful not to allow the fabric to come in contact with the water. This works well for creases in the back of dresses, etc.

Wool: This is a natural fibre made from the fleece of sheep. Hand wash sweaters and other knits in cold water with cold water detergent. Rinse several times and do not wring or twist.

Towel blot and dry flat, reshaping as needed.

A to Z Palace
Spot and
Stain Removal Guide

I'm so glad that you feel safe in airing your dirty laundry with me. I am, after all, the Babe of Borax, one of the original Mould-Diggers, the High Priestess of Household Chemicals, the Vixen of Vinegar, the Deaconess of Dry Cleaning, the Goddess of Grease Stains, the Sultaness of Soap, Solvents and Solutions and of course, the Queen of Clean®! And you know what else? I'm not finished yet . . . not until I give you this, my 'all you need to know' spot and stain removal guide, straight from the palace!

Now, a few words of caution before we begin. *Don't* go trying any of these spot removal methods *without* paying heed to my Royal Rules of Stain Removal. Promise?

Royal Rules of Stain Removal

• Test the spot remover on hidden or inconspicuous areas of the fabric before you proceed.

• Approach the stain from the wrong side of the fabric.

Put a pad of paper towelling under the offending spot as you work. This will help to blot the stain.

• Always blot, never rub! Rubbing will spread the spot and harm the fabric.

• Do not iron or apply heat to spots or stains. Heat will set the stain and you will never be able to remove it.

• If you don't know what caused the stain, start with the weakest and simplest stain removal method.

• Make sure to consider the fabric as well as the stain.

• Remember, the faster you react to a spill or a spot, the better your chances are of removing it completely.

• Directing a hair-dryer at a freshly blotted spot will help it to dry without a ring.

• Sometimes you may still need to pretreat using your favourite laundry spotter.

A to Z

ACID: Acid can permanently damage fabrics, so it must be treated immediately. Neutralize acid by flushing the area with cold running water as soon as possible. Next, spread the garment over a pad of paper towels and moisten with ammonia. Dab the spot several times, then flush again with cold water. If you do not have ammonia on hand, apply a paste of cold water and bicarbonate of soda, then flush with water. Repeat this several times, then launder as usual.

Do not use undiluted ammonia on wool or silk, or on any blends containing these fibres. If you have acid on silk or wool you may dilute ammonia with equal parts of cold water and apply as directed above.

ADHESIVE TAPE: Sponge adhesive tape with eucalyptus oil, baby oil or cooking oil. Allow to soak 10 minutes or so, then work in undiluted washing-up liquid and rinse well. Pretreat and launder as usual.

ALCOHOLIC BEVERAGES: These stains will turn brown with age, so it is important to treat them as soon as possible. First, flush the area with cold water or with soda water, then sponge immediately with a cloth barely dampened with warm water and 1 or 2 drops of washing-up liquid. Rinse with cool water and dry the area with a hair-dryer set on medium.

Alcohol is often invisible when it is spilled, but it can oxidize with heat and age, which makes it impossible to remove. Presoak dry alcohol stains in an enzyme solution such as Ace and launder as usual.

If you spill alcohol on a dry-clean-only fabric, sponge with cold water or soda water and then take the garment to the dry cleaner as soon as possible. Make sure to point out the stain.

For beer spills, sponge with a solution of equal parts white vinegar and washing-up liquid, then rinse in warm water.

For treating red and white wine spills, see **Wine.**

ANIMAL HAIR: Removing pet hair from clothes and bedding can be a challenge. Try using a damp sponge and wiping over clothes and bedding, etc. Rinse the sponge frequently to keep it clean. You can also remove hair by putting on rubber gloves and dipping them in water. Simply dip and wipe, dip and wipe. The hair will rinse off easily.

ANTIPERSPIRANTS AND DEODORANTS: Antiperspirants that contain aluminum chloride are acidic and may interact with some fabrics. If colour changes have occurred, try sponging fabric with ammonia. Rinse thoroughly, and remember to dilute ammonia with equal portions of water when spotting wool or silk.

If you want to avoid yellow underarm stains and prevent colour removal, take a bar of Fairy and work it into the underarm of clothes *before* you launder them for the first time, even if you see no visible stain. Work up a good lather between your thumbs and then launder as usual.

You can also try applying surgical spirit to the stain and covering the area with a folded paper towel dampened with alcohol. Keep it moist and let it sit for a few hours prior to laundering.

To treat yellowed areas that have become stiff, apply an enzyme-soaking product. Ace is a good one to try. Make a stiff paste of the powder by mixing it with cold water. Rub it into the stained areas. Next, put the garment in a plastic bag and leave 8 hours or overnight. Wash in very hot water. If dealing with fabrics that can't withstand hot water, drape the underarm area over a sink and pour 1 litre of hot water through the fabric. Launder as usual.

Don't iron over a deodorant stain or you will never be able to remove it.

I have also had success soaking garments with underarm stains in a solution of 1 litre water and 3 tablespoons of Brilliant Bleach™ (see page 32). Soak up to several days if necessary. Brilliant Bleach™ is safe for whites and colourfast garments.

Last-ditch effort: spray the stained area heavily with heated white vinegar, work in laundry borax, roll up in a plastic bag and leave overnight, then launder as usual.

BABY FORMULA: For white clothes, try applying lemon juice to the stains and laying the garment in the sun. Pretreat and launder as usual.

Unseasoned meat tenderizer is also great for removing formula and baby food stains. Make a paste of the tenderizer and cool water, rub it into the stain and let sit for an hour or so before laundering. Meat tenderizer contains an enzyme that breaks down protein stains. Just make sure to use *unseasoned* tenderizer.

Soaking coloured clothes and whites in Brilliant Bleach™ (see page 32) is also effective, although you may have to soak for several days to achieve perfect results on difficult stains. Remember, this bleach is nonchlorine, so it's totally safe for baby things.

BARBEQUE SAUCE: See *Tomato-Based Stains.*

BEVERAGES: Blot beverage spills immediately until you have absorbed all you can, then sponge with clean, warm water and a little borax. (About ½ teaspoon borax to 100 ml water.) Sponge and blot repeatedly and launder as usual.

Also see information under specific beverage stains.

BLOOD (fresh and dried): If you have blood all over your clothes, laundry may not be your biggest problem . . . for those little accidents try the following:

For washable fabrics, soak as soon as possible in salt water or flush with soda water. You can also make a paste of unseasoned meat tenderizer and cold water, and apply it to the stain for a few hours. Wash in cool water and detergent, by hand or machine.

Pouring 3 per cent hydrogen peroxide through the stained area can be effective in many instances. The sooner you do this the more success you will have. Make sure to do this only on washable fabrics, please. Pour the peroxide through the stain, then flush with cold water, pretreat and launder as usual.

Ace and Brilliant Bleach™ both work well on blood. When using Ace, make a paste with cold water and apply to the stain, allowing it to sit for several hours. With Brilliant Bleach™, soak the garment for a significant period of time – anywhere between 1 to 24 hours. Neither of these products will harm colourfast fabrics.

For dry-clean-only fabrics, sprinkle with salt while the blood is still moist, then take to a dry cleaner as soon as possible.

Human saliva will break down fresh bloodstains, so try applying a little of your own saliva to a small spot of blood – this may do the trick.

For a quick fix for fresh bloodstains, apply cornflour to the surface and then flush from the wrong side of the fabric with soapy water. Pretreat and launder as usual.

Blood on leather can be foamed away with 3 per cent hydrogen peroxide. Dab on the peroxide. Let it bubble and then blot. Continue until the blood is removed. Wipe the surface with a damp cloth and dry.

BUTTER OR MARGARINE: Scrape off any solid concentration of butter with a dull edge, such as the back of a knife.

On washable fabrics, work in undiluted washing-up liquid, wash and dry.

If the stain is old, spray it with WD-40 Lubricant® to regenerate the grease, then work in undiluted washing-up liquid and wash in the hottest water possible for that fabric type.

Sponge silks and delicate fabrics with Dylon Stain Remover 3. Allow to air-dry. Repeat if necessary.

Do not iron the fabric until all traces of the grease have been removed. Ironing will set the stain and make it impossible to remove.

Take dry-clean-only fabrics to the dry cleaner as soon as possible. Be sure to identify the stain and its location on the garment.

CANDLE WAX: For candle wax on clothes and table linens, place the article in a plastic bag, place the bag in the freezer and let the wax freeze. Scrape off what you can with a dull, straight edge – the back of a knife or an old credit card works well. Lay brown paper on the ironing board. (Grocery store bags work well. Just make sure that the writing is face down on the ironing board *away* from the fabric – otherwise you may transfer lettering to your garment.) Cover with more brown paper and press with a medium/hot iron, moving the paper like a blotter until you have absorbed every bit of wax you can. Be patient! Blot with Dylon Stain Remover 3 to remove the balance of the grease from the wax.

CHEWING GUM: See *Gum*.

CHOCOLATE: Scrape off all that you can, then soak washable fabrics for 30 minutes in an enzyme prewash solution. Rub detergent into any remaining stain and work well between your thumbs. Rinse the area under forcefully running cold water. If a grease spot remains, sponge the area with dry-cleaning solution such as Dylon Stain Remover 3. Any residual stain should come out during normal washing. If the stain is still visible after washing, soak in Brilliant Bleach™ (see page 32) or combine 100 ml of 3 per cent hydrogen peroxide and 1 teaspoon of clear ammonia and soak the stain for 10 minutes at a time, checking every 10 minutes and resoaking if necessary. Remember, fabrics need to be tested for colourfastness before using peroxide.

For dry-clean-only fabrics, flush the stain with soda water to prevent setting, then sponge the area with Dylon Stain Remover 3. If the stain persists, take it to your dry cleaner.

COFFEE AND TEA (black or with sugar): Blot up all that you can and, if the garment is washable, flush immediately with cold water. Rub detergent into the stain and work well between your thumbs before laundering as usual. If the stain is still visible and you can use hot water on the fabric, spread the stain over the sink, or stretch over a bowl and tie or rubber band in place (like a little trampoline) and sit the bowl in the sink. Cover the stain with laundry borax and pour boiling water through it, circling from the outside of the stain until you have reached the centre. Let soak 30 minutes to an hour and relaunder.

For more delicate fabrics, soak in Brilliant Bleach™ (see page 32).

For sturdy whites, such as knits and T-shirts, dissolve 2 denture-cleaning tablets in warm water and soak the stain for 30 minutes. Check the garment. If the stain is still visible, soak again and launder as usual.

Out at a restaurant? Dip your napkin in water and sprinkle with salt and blot the offending stain.

For stains from lattes and cappuccinos, see **Milk.**

COLA AND SOFT DRINKS: Sponge these spills as soon as possible with a solution of equal parts alcohol and water. On washable clothes, bleach out remaining stains with an equal mixture of 3 per cent hydrogen peroxide and water. Saturate the stain and wait 20 minutes. If the stain is gone, launder as usual. Repeat if the stain remains. You can also soak the fabric in a solution of Brilliant Bleach™ (see page 32) as directed on the container.

Borax is also effective in soft drink/cola removal. Moisten the spot thoroughly and sprinkle with borax, working well between your thumbs. Flush with water and re-treat if necessary.

Getting the stain out as soon as possible is important: cola and soft drinks will discolour fabrics as they oxidize.

COLLAR STAINS: This is for those women whose husbands won't share laundry duty, the women who didn't know that the wedding ring came with a ring around the collar! It's easy to remove, though. Just use some inexpensive shampoo! Shampoo dissolves body oils so it works great on that collar ring. Keep some in a bottle with a dispenser top in the laundry room. Squirt on enough to cover the offending stain and work it in well, then launder as usual.

COPIER TONER (powder): First, carefully shake off any loose powder and brush lightly with a soft brush. An old, soft toothbrush works well. Pretreat with your favourite spotter or try Spot Shot Instant Carpet Stain Remover® and launder as usual, using the hottest water for the fabric type. Don't rub or brush with your hand. The oil in your skin will spread and set the stain.

COSMETICS (foundation, blusher, eye shadow, eyeliner and mascara): Bar soap such as Dove® and other such beauty bars work well on cosmetics spots. Wet the stain and rub with the soap, working it in well. Flush with warm water and, once the stain is removed, launder as usual.

Sometimes just working in laundry detergent will be all you need. For difficult cases, add some borax to the area and work well between your thumbs.

If your garment is dry clean only, try some Dylon Stain Remover 3 directly on the spot. Make sure to use a cool hair-dryer to keep a ring from forming on the fabric. You'll need to take the garment to a professional cleaner if the stain doesn't come out. (See also *Makeup.*)

CRAYON AND COLOURED PENCIL: Place the stained area on a pad of paper towels and spray with WD-40 Lubricant®. Let stand for a few minutes, then turn the fabric over and spray the other side. Let sit for a further 10 minutes before working undiluted washing-up liquid into the stained area to remove the crayon and oil. Replace the paper-towelling pad as necessary. Wash in the hottest possible water for the fabric, along with your normal detergent and appropriate bleaching agent (depending on whether the clothes are white or coloured). Wash on the longest wash cycle available, and rinse well.

Another way to remove crayon from washable fabrics such as wool, acrylic, linen, cotton and polyester is to lay the offending stain between two pieces of brown paper and press with a warm/medium iron. A grocery bag works well – just remember to keep any ink that may be on the bag away from the fabric. The paper works as a blotter to absorb the crayon, so keep changing it as the wax is absorbed. If any colour mark remains, soak the garment in Brilliant Bleach™ (see page 32) or flush with Universal 2000 De-solv-it. This is a spray stain remover that can also be used as a pre-wash.

Note: Don't panic if the crayon has also gone through the dryer. Simply spray an old rag with WD-40 Lubricant®, then thoroughly wipe down the drum. Make sure the dryer is empty when you do this – no clothes, no crayons. Place a load of dry rags in the dryer and run through a drying cycle when you're through. This will remove any oily residue.

DYE (see also *Hair Dye*): Dye stains are difficult if not impossible to remove. Try one or all of these methods.

Spread the stained area over a bowl and put a rubber band around the fabric *and* the bowl to hold the fabric taut, like a trampoline. Sit the bowl in the sink with the plug out to allow the water to run freely away. Turn on the cold water tap to a nice steady drip and let it drip through the dye spot for 3 to 6 hours. Monitor the sink to be sure the water is draining. This treatment is effective in many cases.

You can also try saturating the dye spot with a combination of equal parts 3 per cent hydrogen peroxide and water. Sit the fabric in the sun, keeping it moist with the solution until the spot completely disappears. Rinse well and launder as usual. Use only on colourfast clothes.

If your dye problem is caused from fugitive colour – that is, colour that has run from one fabric to another during the wash cycle – all the bleaching in the world won't help. Try Dylon Colour Safe Colour Run Remover instead.

Dylon Colour Safe Colour Run Remover is extremely effective on cotton fabrics. It is not for delicates or some blends, so do read the box with care. It may also cause damage to buttons and, in some cases, zips. You may want to remove these prior to treating.

EGG: First scrape off any solid matter. Then, soak the fabric in a glass or plastic container with any enzyme-soaking product, such as Ace. Soak for at least 6 hours or overnight. If a stain remains, work in powder detergent, rubbing vigorously between your thumbs. Rinse and wash as usual. Check the garment carefully for any remaining stain when you remove it from the washing machine. Don't apply heat until all of the stain is removed or the stain will become permanent.

You can also try treating the area with cool water and unseasoned meat tenderizer. Work this into the area well, and allow it to sit for a few hours, being sure to keep the area moist. Continue treating until no stain remains.

Take nonwashables to the dry cleaner as soon as possible. Quick treatment is important. Make sure you identify the stain to your cleaner so it can be treated properly and promptly.

EYELINER AND EYE SHADOW: See *Cosmetics.*

FABRIC SOFTENER SPOTS: For the greasy spots that sometimes appear on clothes after drying with dryer fabric softener sheets, dampen the spot and rub with pure bar soap and relaunder.

For spots from liquid fabric softener, rub with undiluted washing-up liquid and relaunder.

FELT TIP MARKER: See *Marker.*

FOOD DYE: Fruit juices, gelatin desserts, fruit smoothies and frozen fruit sticks all contain food dye that can leave a nasty stain on clothes.

Treating the stain while it is still fresh is the very best thing you can do. If you are out in public and don't have access to any cleaning supplies, wet the spot with soda water or cool water and blot, blot, blot. If you are at home, then treat the spot with 250 ml of cool water to which you have added 1 tablespoon of ammonia. Once you have flushed the spot well with this solution, grab the salt shaker and rub salt into the wound . . . I mean stain! Let this sit for an hour or so, and then brush off the salt. If the stain is still visible, re-treat the same way.

You can also try stretching the fabric tight and holding it

under a forceful stream of cold water. This will flush out much of the spot without spreading it. Next, rub in your favourite detergent, scrubbing vigorously between your thumbs. Rinse again in cool water. Do not apply heat to the stain until it is completely removed.

I have had great success soaking food dye spills in Brilliant Bleach™ (see page 32), just follow the directions for hand-soaking on the container.

Remember, if the stain is not removed during the spotting process, it will not come out in the laundry!

FRUIT AND FRUIT JUICE (also see *Berries*): These stains absolutely must be removed before the fabric is washed. The combination of heat and age will set fruit stains and they will be impossible to remove, even for the Queen.

Sponge or spray the area immediately with soda water or seltzer. If these products aren't available, use cold water. *Do not use hot water.* Rinse the offending spot as soon as possible while it is still wet. Rub in your favourite detergent and scrub the area between your thumbs. *Now* rinse under hot running water – as hot as the fabric can tolerate. Pull the fabric taut and allow the full force of the water to flow through the area. The stronger the flow the better.

If the stain is still visible after this treatment, make a paste of laundry borax and warm water, and work it into the stained area. Let this dry and brush off. Repeat as needed. You can also try pulling the fabric tight over a bowl, using a rubber band to secure it. Sprinkle laundry borax over the stain and, using the hottest water possible for the fabric type, start at the outside edge of the stain and pour the water through the borax in circles until you are pouring through the centre of the stain.

Fresh fruit stains, if treated promptly, will usually come

out. Quick treatment is especially important for fruits such as peach and citrus.

Old Fruit Stains: Before you can remove the stain you must reconstitute it. You can do this by applying glycerin to the area. Rub it in well and allow to soak for 30 minutes. Treat as above.

For nonwashable fabrics, gently sponge the stain with cold water as soon as it occurs and then take to a dry cleaner as quickly as possible. Be sure to identify the stain so it can be treated properly.

If the stains are red in nature, use Wine Away Red Wine Stain Remover™ as directed in the section on berry stains.

FURNITURE POLISH: Furniture polish is usually an oil-based stain, so it must be reconstituted. Restore the oil in the polish by spraying with WD-40 Lubricant®. Allow the lubricant to soak for 10 minutes, then work in undiluted washing-up liquid. Work this in well between your thumbs to remove the grease. Flush with a forceful stream of the hottest water you can for the fabric type.

You can also try cleaning the area with Dylon Stain Remover or Universal 2000 De-solv-it, used according to can directions.

If the furniture polish has colour in it, refer to the section on dye.

GLUE, ADHESIVES, MUCILAGE: Modern adhesives and glues are very hard to remove. You may have to use a special solvent. Take the garment to the dry cleaner and be sure to identify the spot.

Here's a rundown of glue types and how to remove them.

Model Glue: Can usually be removed with nail polish remover containing acetone, although you may need to pur-

chase straight acetone at the hardware store or the chemist.
Always test the acetone in a small area first.

Plastic Adhesives: For best results, treat these stains before
they dry. Try washing in cool water and detergent. If the
stain remains, bring 250 ml or so of white vinegar to a boil,
and immerse the stain. Have more vinegar boiling as you
treat the stain so that you can switch to the hot vinegar as
soon as the first amount starts to cool. Continue reheating
the vinegar and treating for 15 to 20 minutes.

Rubber Cement: Scrape off all that you can with a dull,
straight edge that you can throw away. (Don't use a credit
card for this – unless it's over its limit!) Treat with Universal
2000 De-solv-it as directed.

You can also try working petroleum jelly into the glue
until it pills into balls that you can then scrape from the fabric. Treat the area with undiluted washing-up liquid and
launder in the hottest water the fabric will tolerate.

Miscellaneous Glues: Sponge or rinse the fabric in warm
water. Work in your favourite powdered detergent or liquid
detergent along with some laundry borax. Rub vigorously
between your thumbs. Rinse and wash in the hottest water
you can for the fabric type.

Remember, soap and water will remove most synthetic
glue when the spot is fresh. Acetone will remove most clear,
plastic cement-type glues. Make sure to test acetone in an
inconspicuous area, and never use on acetate fabrics – it will
dissolve them.

For old, dried glue stains, soak the fabric in a solution of
boiling hot white vinegar and water. Use 2 parts white vinegar to every 10 parts of water and soak for 30 to 60 minutes.
You may need to scrape off the glue as it softens. Then pretreat and launder as usual.

GRASS, FLOWERS AND FOLIAGE: There are several ways to remove grass stains from fabrics. Pick one and try it. If it doesn't completely remove the stain, try another. Don't put clothes into the dryer until the grass stain is removed.

First a word of caution: avoid using alkalis such as ammonia, degreasers or alkaline detergents. They interact with the tannin in the grass stains and may permanently set the stain.

Okay – first, washable fabrics: Sponge on rubbing alcohol, repeating several times. If the stain persists, sponge with white vinegar and rinse. Work in your favourite laundry detergent and rinse well.

Rubbing white nongel toothpaste into grass stains will often remove them. Rub well, then rinse and wash as usual.

For jeans, apply undiluted surgical spirit (i.e. rubbing alcohol) to the area and allow to soak 15 minutes before laundering as usual.

Spot Shot Carpet Stain Remover® also works very well on grass stains. Follow the label directions.

For grass on white leather shoes, rub the grass stain with treacle and leave it on the shoe overnight. Wash the treacle off with hot soap and water, and the grass stain should be gone.

For grass on suede fabric, including shoes, rub the stain with a sponge dipped in glycerin. Then rub with a cloth dipped in undiluted white vinegar, brush the nap gently to reset, and allow to dry and brush again. Remember: test in an inconspicuous spot first.

GRAVY: With gravy you need to remove the starch used to thicken it, so you will want to soak the garment in cold water long enough to dissolve the starch. It may take several hours.

Pretreat prior to laundering with a good spotter, such as Spot Shot Carpet Stain Remover®. Launder in the hottest possible water for the fabric type.

You can also soak the garment in Brilliant Bleach™ (see page 32), for days if necessary.

GREASE AND OIL (including cooking oil and salad dressing): Grease and oil must be removed thoroughly, otherwise a semitransparent stain will set and will turn dark from all the soil it attracts.

To treat a grease stain it helps to know whether it is from animal oil, vegetable oil or motor oil.

To remove a grease stain, first remove as much of the greasy substance as possible without forcing the grease further down into the fabric fibres. Use a paper towel to blot and absorb all the grease that you can. Next, apply a drawing agent such as bicarbonate of soda, cornflour, or talcum powder. Rub it in gently and let it sit for 15 to 30 minutes to allow the agent to absorb and draw the grease out of the fabric. Brush the powder off thoroughly and check the stain. If it looks like you can absorb more grease, repeat the process.

Next, lay the fabric over a thick rag or a heavy fold of paper towels. Working from the back of the fabric, blot with Dylon Stain Remover. Change the pad under the fabric as needed and repeat if necessary.

When grease stains are stubborn, we need to fall back on the idea that grease removes grease. Spray the grease spot with WD-40 Lubricant® and let it soak for 10 minutes, then work in undiluted washing-up liquid and work well between your thumbs. Flush with the hottest water you can for the fabric, pretreat and launder as usual. Do not use this method on silk or crease-resistant finishes.

Many grease stains will eventually turn yellow when set with age and heat. Treat these stains by soaking in diluted hydrogen peroxide or Brilliant Bleach™ (see page 32). Don't use this process unless you know that the clothes are colourfast.

Use Dylon Stain Remover 3 on dry-clean-only fabrics, or take to a professional dry cleaner.

For heavily soiled, greasy work clothes, try pouring a can of original Coca-Cola® in the washing machine with your detergent and launder as usual. The combination of sugar and cola syrup works wonders!

GUM: The best way to deal with gum is to harden it first. Harden any item marred by chewing gum by placing it in a plastic bag in the freezer and leaving it overnight. Immediately upon removing the bag from the freezer, scrape off any gum that you can with a dull straight edge. If all the gum is removed, treat the fabric with an equal mixture of white vinegar and washing-up liquid. You may also try treating the area with lighter fluid, although you must do this outside and use extreme care, testing the fabric first.

Sometimes rubbing the area with egg white (*not* the yolk – no joke!) will remove the remaining residue.

If gum is still trapped, try working petroleum jelly into the fibres, and scraping off the little balls that form. Be sure to follow the directions under **Grease** in this section to remove the grease from the petroleum jelly.

Petroleum jelly will also soften old, dry gum. You want to work the petroleum jelly into the gum and then scrape off all that you can.

For those of you who ask, yes, peanut butter will work too, but it is messier. My advice is to eat the peanut butter and use the petroleum jelly!

For dry-clean-only fabrics, you may freeze the fabric and

scrape off what gum you can. Take it to your dry cleaner right away.

HAIR DYE: If you didn't listen to me when I told you to dye your hair naked in the garden, then hair-dye spots may be a major problem for you. Here's what to do:

Clothing or fabrics stained with hair dye should be washed in warm water, to which you have added white vinegar and your normal detergent. Do this in a sink or container, adding about 2 tablespoons of detergent and 500 ml white vinegar to 3.8 litres warm water. Let it soak for several hours.

If the stain still remains, try our favorite bleach, Brilliant Bleach™ (see page 32). You can soak whites and colourfast fabrics for several days if necessary, without damage. Try to avoid the hair dye problem if you can. I suggest using the same old towel when you do your hair.

HAND CREAM: Blot off all that you can and treat with Dylon Stain Remover, working from the back of the fabric. Once all of the stain is removed, launder as usual.

ICE CREAM: Yummy-yummy in the tummy – not so great on clothes! Sponge the garment as quickly as possible with cold water, soda water or seltzer. If a stain still remains, treat it with cold water and unseasoned meat tenderizer. Let this soak on the fabric for about 30 minutes or so and then flush with cold water to see if the offending spot is gone. Pretreat with Spot Shot Carpet Stain Remover® and launder as usual.

If a grease spot remains, treat with Dylon Stain Remover, working from the back of the fabric over a pad of paper towels to absorb the spot and the spotting solution.

Sometimes treating ice cream-stained fabric with a small

amount of ammonia will also work. Then, of course, launder as usual.

INK: How can one little pen cause so much grief? The first line of offence is rubbing alcohol. Sponge the ink mark, or dip it into a glass of rubbing alcohol, letting it soak until the offending spot is removed. Don't be tricked into using hair spray. That may have worked in the past, but hair spray now contains a lot of oil, and that just spreads the stain.

You also can try using acetone. This too must be tested. (And remember, *never* use acetone on acetates.)

White, nongel toothpaste rubbed firmly and vigorously into the stain may work. After this method be sure to pre-treat and launder as usual.

Often just soaking ink stains in milk will dissolve them.

Turpentine is effective on very challenging ink stains. Working over a pad of paper towels, tap the spot on the back of the fabric using the back of a spoon or an old toothbrush. Don't rub. Work in undiluted washing-up liquid prior to laundering, and wash in the hottest water possible for the fabric type. Dispose of all paper, etc., saturated with turpentine immediately – outside, please.

Some inks only respond to solvents, so you may need to use Stain Devil 4.

On leather, remove ballpoint ink by rubbing with cuticle remover or petroleum jelly. You may need to leave it on the stained area for several days to achieve success.

On vinyl, believe it or not, the best thing is for you to be so mad that you could spit! Saliva will remove ballpoint ink from vinyl – as long as you are quick. Apply generously and wipe with a soft cloth. For old stains, apply glycerin, let it soak for 30 minutes or so, and then attempt to wash the stain away with a wet soft cloth rubbed over a bar of soap.

KETCHUP: See *Tomato-Based Stains.*

LIPSTICK: Lipstick is actually an oily dye stain. Water, heat or wet spotters will only spread it and make the problem worse and set the stain.

Rub in vegetable oil, WD-40 Lubricant® or liquid paraffin, and let it sit on the spot for 15 to 30 minutes. Next sponge the area with a little ammonia – sudsy or clear is fine.

Now, before you launder, work in undiluted washing-up liquid to be sure you have removed all of the oil.

In an emergency, try spraying the spot with a little hair spray. Let this sit for a few minutes and then wipe gently with a damp cloth. Test this method in an inconspicuous spot first.

You will also find that Spot Shot Carpet Stain Remover® is generally effective on lipstick.

If you are getting dressed and you accidentally get lipstick on your clothes, try rubbing the stain with white bread. (Yes, it has to be white!)

MAKEUP (oily foundation, powder, cream blush, concealer creams): Sprinkle bicarbonate of soda on the makeup smudge, then brush the area with an old wet toothbrush until the makeup is removed. Nongel white toothpaste scrubbed with a toothbrush is also effective.

Washing-up liquid or shampoo will generally remove makeup stains. Work the product into the stain vigorously between your thumbs.

For stubborn makeup stains use nonoily makeup remover, pretreat and launder as usual. (See also *Cosmetics.*)

MARKER, PERMANENT: First of all, permanent usually means permanent. But before you give up and throw in the towel – or blouse or trousers or whatever – here are some things to try.

If the stain appears stubborn, try scrubbing the marker spot with an old toothbrush, white, nongel toothpaste, and some bicarbonate of soda. Give it a really good scrubbing. Rinse. If the marker stain is almost gone, soak in 250 ml warm water and 2 denture-cleaning tablets for whites, and Brilliant Bleach™ (see page 32) for colourfast clothes. This will require some time, but the stain all comes out, so it's worth it.

If the marker is still there, scrub with Lava™ soap prior to trying the denture-cleaning tablets or bleach.

MARKER, WASHABLE: Rinse the stain from the fabric with cold water until no more colour can be removed. Place the fabric on paper towels and saturate the back of the fabric with alcohol, using a cotton wool ball to blot the stain. Replace the paper towels as needed as they absorb the colour. Work in Fairy Mild Green Household Soap until the spot is well lathered and wash in hot water with laundry detergent and fabric appropriate bleach. Rinse in warm water.

MAYONNAISE: See *Grease.*

MEAT JUICES: Once dry, meat juices are very tough to remove, so it's important to react quickly. Sponge the area immediately with cold water (not hot – it will set the stain), or with soda water. Next, apply unseasoned meat tenderizer and cold water, working the mixture in well. Let it sit for 30 to 60 minutes. Pretreat and launder as usual, but be sure to use *cool* water.

On dry-clean-only fabrics, sponge with cold water and take to a professional cleaner.

MEDICINES: It would be impossible to list all the medicines on the market. But this section should give you an idea of what to look out for, as well as what to do for each family of medicine.

Alcohol: Medicines containing alcohol stain quickly. Treat these stains as you would spilled alcohol.

Iron: Iron or medicines containing iron products should be treated as rust.

Oily Medicines: Oily medicines should be treated with a degreasing product. I have had great luck with Soapworks At Home All-Purpose Cleaner™ (see page 31), used undiluted. Work it in well and then rinse.

You can also treat these stains as you would an oil or grease stain.

Syrups: Cough syrup or children's medicines can usually be removed with water. Soak the fabric with cool water as soon as possible. Running cold water full force through the fabric can be helpful, and you may also want to try working in Fairy Mild Green Household Soap, or soaking the stain in Ace or Brilliant Bleach™ (see page 32).

MILDEW: Mildew is a fungus that grows and flourishes in warm, humid, dark conditions, like the shower, the basement, etc. The best way to avoid mildew is to ensure that things are totally dry *before* you put them away. Invisible spores can quickly grow to huge proportions, especially on natural materials such as cotton, wool, leather, paper, wood, etc.

Air needs to circulate to keep mildew from forming, so do not crowd clothes into cupboards.

Store clothing only after it has been cleaned and dried thoroughly.

If you are storing things such as leather purses, belts, shoes, even suitcases, clean them well, then sit them in the sun for an hour or so. Do not store things in plastic as this caters to damp conditions.

If you smell a damp or musty smell coming from a cupboard, suspect mildew immediately and act quickly to dry it out. Even allowing a fan to blow in the cupboard overnight can make a huge difference by drying and circulating the air.

Okay – here's what to do if you already have mildew stains on fabrics. First, try working some Fairy Mild Green Household Soap into the area and laundering. If stains remain and the fabric will tolerate chlorine bleach, soak it in 3.8 litres cold water to which you have added 2 to 3 tablespoons of chlorine (household) bleach.

Moistening white or colourfast clothes with lemon juice, sprinkling them with salt and laying the garment in the sun may also remove mildew. If in doubt, test this method first.

Leather presents a different challenge. Take the item outside and brush off all the powdery mildew that you can with a soft brush. Wipe the leather with equal parts of rubbing alcohol and water, or try massaging cuticle remover into the area. After 10 minutes, wipe vigorously with a soft cloth.

Wash leather with a complexion bar soap such as Dove® and buff dry – do not rinse.

Remember: with mildew, the best defence is a good offence, so try to keep it from occurring.

MILK/CREAM: Rinse fabric under a cold, forceful stream of water from the tap. Treat with unseasoned meat tenderizer and cool water. Allow to soak for 30 minutes, then flush with cool water again. If greasy-looking marks remain, treat with Dylon Stain Remover, working from the back of the fabric over a heavy pad of paper towels. Launder as usual.

Treat washable fabrics stained from milk by flushing with cool water before working in detergent and a little ammonia. Wash in cool water and air-dry.

For dry-clean-only fabrics, take to a professional as soon as possible and identify the stain when you drop off the item.

MUD: The key word here is *dry*. Let mud dry. Never treat a wet mud stain other than lifting off any solid pieces with a dull straight edge. Once mud has dried, take the vacuum cleaner and vacuum the area with the hose attachment. You'll achieve the greatest suction that way. This may be a two-person job. One to hold the fabric, one to hold the hose.

Rub the cut side of a potato over the mud stain and launder as usual.

For stubborn stains, sponge with equal portions of rubbing alcohol and cool water. For red mud stains, treat with a rust remover. (See **Rust**). Rubbing laundry borax into a dampened mud stain will often remove it.

Spraying with Spot Shot Carpet Stain Remover® prior to laundering is also helpful.

MUSTARD: The word makes me shiver! This is a terrible stain to attempt (notice I said *attempt*) to remove.

The turmeric in mustard is what gives mustard its distinctive bright yellow colour – it's also what would make it a darn good dye!

Remove as much of the mustard as possible, using a dull straight edge. Next, flex the fabric to break the grip of the embedded residue on the fabric fibres. Apply glycerin (available from chemists) and let it sit at least an hour. Pretreat and launder as usual.

If the fabric is white or colourfast, soak the stain in hydrogen peroxide for 30 minutes. Again, Brilliant Bleach™ (see page 32) may remove the stain after a lengthy soaking.

For white clothes, dissolve a denture-cleaning tablet in 100 ml cool water and allow the stained area to soak.

Things to avoid: ammonia and heat. They will both set the stain and you will never get it out.

Kind of makes you think that ketchup and relish are all you need on that hotdog, doesn't it!

MYSTERY STAINS: These are spots and spills that you have no idea where they came from. The unknowns. Here's what to do:

• Blot with cool water (hot water sets stains).

• Blot with a sponge or cloth dampened with water and a teaspoon or so of white vinegar (not for cotton or linen).

• Blot with a sponge or cloth dampened with water and a teaspoon or so of clear ammonia (again, not for cotton or linen).

• Blot with surgical spirit diluted 50/50 with cool water.

• Sponge with a solution of Brilliant Bleach™ (see page 32) and water.

NAIL POLISH: Okay, if you had polished your nails naked in the garden you wouldn't be reading this, would you? Stretch the fabric over a glass bowl and make a little trampoline by securing the fabric with a rubber band. Drip acetone-based polish remover through the stain with a stainless steel spoon (not silver) and tap the stain with the edge of the spoon. Continue dripping the acetone through the fabric until the polish is removed. This requires time and patience. If you run out of either, walk away and come back later. Straight acetone, purchased from chemists, may work faster, but be sure to test an area first.

If a colour stain remains after the polish is removed, dilute hydrogen peroxide (50 per cent peroxide, 50 per cent water) apply to the stain, and sit the fabric in the sun, keeping it moist with the peroxide solution. Do this only for white or colourfast clothes.

Do not use acetone on silk or acetates, and always test the acetone on an inconspicuous area prior to beginning.

Nonwashable fabrics should be dry-cleaned.

ODOURS: Eliminate odours, don't use a perfumed cover-up. I like ODORZOUT™ (see page 48) odour eliminator because it absorbs odours and removes them permanently – without leaving any telltale smells behind. It is nontoxic and safe for all surfaces, and it can be used wet or dry. It is also safe for the environment and a little goes a long way. Keep some on hand. It's great for just about any odour you're likely to come across, such as smoke, mildew, mould, feces, urine, food odours, any kind of odour. Do not use a perfumed cover-up.

OIL (also see *Grease and Oil***):** Blot up all oil quickly. Avoid rubbing or you will force the oil further into the fibres. Pretreat washable fabrics with your favourite spot remover, or use one recommended for oily stains in this book. Launder in the hottest possible water for the fabric.

Nonwashables should be dry-cleaned.

OINTMENT (zinc oxide, Sudocrem, zinc and castor oil): Anyone who has had a baby will be familiar with this problem stain.

Use hot water and detergent, rubbing the fabric against itself to remove the oil. If the stain remains, treat as indicated in the section on *Grease and Oil*.

For zinc oxide, soak the garment in white vinegar for 30 minutes after treating as above, then launder as usual.

PAINT, LATEX: Treat this stain immediately for best results. It is important to remove paint *before* it dries, so keep the stain wet if you can't work on it right away.

Flush the paint from the fabric with a forceful stream of warm water. Next, treat the stain with a solution of washing-up liquid and water, or laundry detergent and water. Work it into the stained area, soaping and rinsing until the stain is removed. Do this as many times as necessary. If the fabric is colourfast, you can also work in some dishwasher detergent and let it soak on the fabric for 5 to 10 minutes before laundering as usual.

On fabrics such as cotton and polyester, try spraying the garment with oven cleaner and letting it sit about 15 to 30 minutes before flushing with plenty of water. Use *extreme* care with this method and use it at your own risk. Some fabrics cannot tolerate the oven cleaner, but if the garment is ruined by the paint, it is worth a try. Also use care where you spray the oven cleaner and what you sit the fabric on afterwards.

PAINT, OIL-BASED: Get busy and remove this spill ASAP. You're out of luck if it dries. If you must go to the store for products, keep the spill moist: *Do not allow oil-based paint to dry.*

Check the paint can and use the thinner recommended by the manufacturer. Sometimes thinner for correction fluid will also work. Remember to test an area first with these two methods.

When working on a paint spill, work from the back of the

fabric over a thick pad of paper towels. Tap the stained area with an old toothbrush or an old spoon as you work to force the paint out.

Now that you have removed the stain, saturate it with detergent and work in vigorously. Cover the area with the hottest water you can use for the fabric, and let it soak overnight. Scrub again, between your thumbs, and launder as usual.

PENCIL: Okay, how easy is this? Take a nice, clean, soft eraser, and gently rub the offending mark away! Just be sure the eraser is clean, or you will create a large stain. If the spot is stubborn, sponge with Stain Devil.

PERFUME: Follow the directions in the section on *Alcoholic Beverages.* A few words to the wise: the best time to put it on is right before you put on your clothes, not after. And never spray perfume directly on your clothes. This will damage them. The combination of alcohol and oil is death to fabrics.

PERSPIRATION STAINS: These stains really are the pits, so I've devoted an entire chapter to their removal. Also check out the section in this stain removal guide on *Antiperspirants and Deodorants.*

PLAY DOUGH: First of all, let gravity do the work for you. Lay the fabric over a bowl and let it simply drop off. You'll only have to clean up what's left!

Scrape off the balance of any play dough with a dull edge such as an old credit card or knife back. Spray with WD-40 Lubricant® and let stand a few minutes. Scrape again, removing all the play dough that you can. Continue to do this, changing from the dull straight edge to cotton wool balls. If any stain remains, saturate a cotton wool ball with rubbing alcohol, blot the stain, and rinse. Work in washing-up liquid and launder as usual in the hottest water you can for the fabric type.

If you don't have WD-40 Lubricant®, use petroleum jelly instead.

RUST: On white fabrics, saturate with lemon juice and sprinkle with salt, then lay in the sun. (No, not you – the fabric!) If the rust is stubborn, apply the lemon juice and salt, and pour water through the stain. Use boiling water if the fabric will tolerate it; otherwise use hot. Check the care label.

You can also cover the stained area with cream of tartar, then gather up the edges of the fabric and dip the spot in hot water. Let stand 5 to 10 minutes and then launder as usual.

SAP, PINE TAR: See *Tar*.

SCORCH MARKS: Sorry to say, but severe scorch marks cannot be removed.

Light scorch marks may be treated with a cloth dampened with 1 part 3 per cent hydrogen peroxide and 3 parts of water. Lay the cloth over the scorch mark and press with a medium/hot iron. Do not iron off of the cloth or you will scorch the fabric again. Make sure to try this method first in a small, inconspicuous space.

If the scorch is still visible, moisten the spot with the diluted peroxide and lay it in the sun.

Very light scorch marks may also be removed by wetting them with water and laying the garment in the sun.

If the scorch mark has appeared on white clothes, saturate the scorched area with lemon juice and lay it in the sun. Keep it moist with the lemon juice until the stain is removed.

For white cottons, sometimes boiling in 55 g soap flakes

and 2 litres milk will remove the stain. Try this at your own risk. Some fabrics may not tolerate boiling.

For light scorches you can also rub the fabric with the cut side of a white onion (not a red onion – it will stain) and then soak the fabric in cold water for several hours. Launder as usual.

Remember: scorching weakens fibres, so use care and always relaunder the item once the scorch mark has been removed.

SHOE POLISH: Work laundry detergent into the fabric immediately and rinse. For persistent stains, sponge with alcohol. Use surgical spirit (i.e. rubbing alcohol) on white clothes, and 1 part alcohol to 2 parts water on coloured fabrics. Rinse again, or try using turpentine after first testing in an inconspicuous spot.

Shoe polish has an oily base containing dye. Using the wrong things such as water, heat or wet spotters will spread and set the stain. Work in vegetable oil or WD-40 Lubricant® and let it sit for 15 minutes. Sponge on a little ammonia (not on silk, please), then work in undiluted washing-up liquid and launder as usual.

Dylon Stain Remover may also help to eliminate the final stained area.

If you have any discoloration remaining from the dye in the shoe polish, soak the fabric in Brilliant Bleach™ (see page 32) until the stain is removed.

If the shoe polish stain is old and heavy, you may need to treat it with petroleum jelly. Cover the polish and work in the petroleum jelly, let it soak for 30 to 60 minutes, and then scrape off all that you can of the polish and the petroleum jelly. Work in undiluted washing-up liquid and flush with a forceful stream of hot water. Pretreat and launder as usual.

Liquid Shoe Polish: Blot up all that you can from the fabric. Do not rub – this will spread the stain. Do not apply water. Instead, saturate with surgical spirits (i.e. rubbing alcohol) – undiluted for whites, diluted as above for colours. Continue to flush with surgical spirits, work in your favourite laundry detergent, then rub vigorously to remove all trace of the stain.

SILK SPOTS: Spots on silk are hard to remove and must be handled with care.

Dry-cleaning solvent may spot-clean silk, but you're likely to be left with a ring on the fabric. Make sure to use the hair-dryer on the spot to avoid that telltale ring.

For unusual or heavy stains, take to a professional. Too much rubbing can remove the colour from silk.

SOFT DRINKS: See *Colas and Soft Drinks.*

SOOT: Launder clothing in the hottest possible water for the fabric with your normal detergent, 115 g laundry borax and 115 g soda crystals.

STICKERS: Heat white vinegar and apply it, undiluted, directly to the fabric. Allow the vinegar to soak until the sticker can be peeled back with ease.

SWEETS: To remove sweets from fabrics, combine 1 table-spoon washing-up liquid with 1 tablespoon white vinegar and 1 litre warm water. Soak the stain in it for 15 to 30 minutes, then flush with warm, clear water. Pretreat and launder as usual.

For chocolate stains, see *Chocolate.*

TAR: Lift off as much solid matter as possible using a plastic (disposable) knife. Spread the stained area over a heavy pad of paper towels and apply glycerin to the fabric, tapping it with the back of an old toothbrush or plastic spoon. Change the paper towels as they absorb the tar. Finally, once you have removed all the tar you can, work in some turpentine or eucalyptus oil. Flush the stained area with surgical spirit (i.e. rubbing alcohol), or work in undiluted washing-up liquid. Pretreat and launder as usual. Spot Shot Carpet Stain Remover® is a good spotter for this.

Dried Tar: Warm the glycerin or some olive oil and spread over the area, allowing it to soak until the tar is loosened. Then proceed as above.

Nonwashables should be taken to the dry cleaner as soon as possible.

TEA: See *Coffee and Tea.*

TOMATO-BASED STAINS (ketchup, spaghetti sauce, tomato sauce, barbecue sauce, etc.): Flush these stains well with cool water as soon as possible. Make sure you apply water to the back of the fabric. Apply white vinegar and then flush again with a forceful stream of water.

If stain persists there are commercial stain removers designed to deal with specific marks.

URINE: Fresh urine stains are fairly easy to remove. First rinse well, flushing with lots of cool water. Presoak using an enzyme powder or Ace. Then launder as usual.

You may also soak urine-stained fabric in salt water, then rinse and launder as usual.

If the colour of the fabric has changed due to the urine, sponge the area or spray with clear ammonia, then rinse and launder as usual.

For Old Urine Stains: Soak in clear hot water for an hour – the hotter the better. Add detergent and wash as usual, then rinse. Use the appropriate bleach for the fabric type, or Brilliant Bleach™ (see page 32) if you prefer.

See also the treatment mentioned under **Odours**.

VOMIT: Shake off or scrape what you can over the toilet. Flush the fabric from the wrong side with cool water, using a forceful stream. Once you have removed solid matter and excess liquid, make a paste of liquid laundry soap and borax and vigorously scrub the fabric. Rinse with salt water, pretreat and launder as usual.

Quick treatment is important to avoid stains from foods and stomach acid.

See also the treatment mentioned for **Odours**.

WINE: Never serve red wine without having white wine nearby! And always tend to the stain *as soon as you can!*

For red wine spills, dilute the spot with white wine, then flush with cool water and apply salt.

If no white wine is available, sprinkle heavily with salt and flush with soda water or cool water.

Applying a paste of laundry borax and water usually works.

YELLOW SPOTS AND STAINS: These stains are common on white clothes and linens. Denture-cleaning tablets will generally remove these stains. Fill a basin with water and add one or two tablets. Allow the tablets to dissolve and then soak the fabric until the yellow is removed.

Resource Guide

ACE: This 'wash booster' contains 5–15 per cent oxygen bleaching agents and can also be used on delicate fabrics such as wool and silk. Available at supermarkets.

ACETONE: A great spotter, but be careful. It is exceedingly strong and can damage fibres. Look for this at chemists and hardware stores.

ACT NATURAL CLOTHS®: See Euronet USA.

BORAX: A laundry additive (sometimes called domestic borax) that can be found at chemists.

BRILLIANT BLEACH™: See Soapworks.

CLEAR AMMONIA: There are two types of ammonia, clear and sudsy (sometimes called 'cloudy'). Clear doesn't contain soap and should be used where suggested for that reason.

DYLON: They have a great range of products all available at supermarkets. The Dylon Colour Seal works on most washable fabrics to seal in colour and they also do a range of colour run removers for both machine and handwashing fabrics. Dylon also do stain removers specific to washable fabrics and some dry clean fabrics with a special applicator to prevent moisture rings.

EPSOM SALTS: Usually used for medicinal purposes, but handy for laundry too. Look for this at the chemists.

EURONET USA: Makers of Act Natural® microfibre cloths. These easy-to-use cloths have been scientifically proven to kill germs and bacteria. They even come with a warranty. I never travel without a cloth, and I keep one in my desk and briefcase to quickly clean up any of those little spills on clothes. Visit their website at: www.euronetusa.com

FAIRY MILD GREEN HOUSEHOLD SOAP: You'll find this wonderful spotter and cleaner in the laundry section of the supermarket.

FRESH BREEZE LAUNDRY SOAP®: See Soapworks.

GLOBRIGHT: A home dry cleaning kit which deoderises clothes and can treat some stains. Available at chemists.

GLYCERIN: Ask for glycerin in chemists. Always purchase plain glycerin, *not* the type containing rosewater.

HYDROGEN PEROXIDE: Make sure to choose 3 per cent – the type used for cuts, *not* the type used to bleach hair. (That's too strong and will remove colour from fabric.)

MEAT TENDERIZER: Great for spotting protein stains. Use the unseasoned variety please, or you will have a whole new stain to deal with. Store brands work fine.

METHYLATED SPIRITS: This is an industrial alcohol reserved for heavy-duty cleaning. Don't use it near an open flame, and make sure to dispose outside the home any rags that were used to apply it. Launder or clean anything that you treat with it as soon as possible. It comes in plastic bottles from hardware stores.

NAIL POLISH REMOVER: I caution you to use nonacetone polish remover first. It's much less aggressive than acetone polish remover.

NONGEL TOOTHPASTE: This is just a fancy name for old-fashioned plain white toothpaste. Gels just don't work, so don't even try.

ODORZOUT®: A fabulous, dry, 100 per cent natural deodorizer. It's nontoxic, so you can use it anyplace you have a smell or a stink. Also available in a pouch for shoes, laundry hampers, etc. Visit their website at: www.88stink.com.

PERSIL REVIVE: This is a home dry cleaning kit for use in the dryer. Not to be used on all fabrics, so read the label carefully. Available at supermarkets.

SHAVING CREAM: The cheaper brands work fine for spotting. Cream works better than gel.

SOAPWORKS: Manufacturer of wonderful nontoxic, user-friendly and earth-friendly cleaning, laundry and personal care products. Try their Fresh Breeze Laundry Powder®, originally designed for allergy and asthma sufferers. Also try their Brilliant Bleach®. Believe me, it *is* brilliant! Visit their website at: www.soapworks.com.

SODA CRYSTALS: A laundry product that can be found in the detergent aisle at the supermarket along with other laundry additives. No, you cannot substitute bicarbonate of soda; it's a different product!

SOOT AND DIRT REMOVAL SPONGE: These big brick erasers are available at hardware stores, usually near the wallpaper supplies. Clean them by washing in a bucket of warm water and washing-up liquid, rinse well, and allow to dry before using again.

SPOT SHOT INSTANT CARPET STAIN REMOVER®: My all-time favorite carpet spotter is a wonderful laundry spotter too! Available at Asda and Londis and some hardware stores.

STAIN DEVILS: A great series of spotters that target specific stains, such as gum, blood, milk, etc.

UNIVERSAL 2000 DE-SOLV-IT: This is a spray stain remover which can be used as a prewash. Available at supermarkets.

WD-40® LUBRICANT: Fine spray oil for lubricating all kinds of things, WD-40® is wonderful for regenerating grease so that it can be removed from clothes. Look for this at the hardware store and even the supermarket.

Index

Your Personal Tips and Hints

Your Personal Tips and Hints

Your Personal Tips and Hints

Your Personal Tips and Hints

POCKET
B O O K S

TALKING DIRTY WITH THE QUEEN OF CLEAN
Linda Cobb

Want to clean a coffeepot in a flash? Unclog a sink with a simple homemade solution? Remove a stubborn stain?

Let Her Royal Highness of housekeeping show you how to turn your home into a sparkling palace – in no time at all! Here comes the Queen of Clean, and her down-to-earth housekeeping guide for those of us who live in the real world and don't want to be a slave to housework.

The Queen counts her pennies too – with inexpensive, environmentally friendly cleaning concoctions and ingredients you might never expect. They include onion (a great rust-remover), lemon juice, vinegar, petroleum jelly, baking soda and tea – the wood cleaner you can drink.

PRICE £6.99
ISBN 0-7434-1582-5